TOP MIND

MENTAL TRAINING FOR AVIATION AND AEROSPACE PROFESSIONALS

Professional Excellence and Top Level Performance Training System

NOEL COX

avcox

www.avcox.com[1]

1. http://www.avcox.com

CONTENTS

Introduction

Hello, I'm excited to have the opportunity to bring you this highly specialized course about mental performance techniques and how they can help you excel in your field. Throughout the years, I've had the privilege to have worked with many world-class high-performing individuals and teams, including top training pilots and other aviation and aerospace professionals around the world and have observed firsthand the power of focus, dedication, and resilience when it comes to achieving excellence in this field.

I've also witnessed and experienced firsthand the unique challenges and stressors that come with working in the aviation and aerospace industries. Jetlag, time away from home, uncertainty, operational issues, commercial concerns, high-pressure situations, and the need for constant attention to detail while balancing your personal and profession lives can all take a toll on your mental and physical wellbeing. It's vital to consider your overall wellbeing when pursuing excellence and improving your performance. The management of mental health and wellbeing while on and off duty needs to be considered a vital safety behavior. By taking care of your mental and physical health, you will be better equipped to handle the challenges that come with your profession. There is a need for more supports and resources focused on this area and until the airlines and aerospace companies provide more robust supports the pilots and astronauts are left to manage these elements themselves, "... *research has led to evidence-based recommendations for interventions to promote wellbeing (including positive mental health and mental wellbeing) in the workplace, both at an airline level and pilot self-management level (including while on and off duty). Overall, airline organizations might increase their support for preventative mental health treatment, and supporting pilot training in relation to adopting healthy behaviors, using specific coping strategies, and risk identifying behavior. (Cahill et al, 2020)…*"[1]

This course helps address those needs, and throughout this course, I will share with you some of the best evidence-based insights, practices and tools I've learned over three decades to help you achieve excellence and improve your performance, all while prioritizing your wellbeing. From techniques to enhance your focus and concentration to strategies for managing stress and building resilience, I will provide you with actionable steps to take your performance to the next level and to enjoy the lifestyle in a healthier and more balanced way. I am continually surprised to find a general lack of information and accessible resources on the mental health and wellbeing aspects of work and lifestyle. It was always just assumed that pilots and astronauts, air traffic controllers and ground personnel simply are born with professionalism and cool calm confidence in their DNA. That they are all simply the right stuff, cut from a different cloth. I'm here to tell you that in my observation this simply is not true; industry professionals are just as human and normal as anyone else, and it is through the highest quality of training and education that the best in the world learn to perform with excellence. Top professional traits are not innate qualities that some people are just born with. They can be developed through intentional and deliberate practice Even those with natural talents and abilities still had to work hard on maintaining wellbeing. They were not born that way, and it takes constant focus and hard work to maintain the quality of professionalism and attention to detail that makes them world class. I can confidently say that the approach in this book is very different to any other out there. I will provide you with practical tools and techniques to help you achieve a state of peak performance and wellbeing and how to operate at the highest levels of professionalism. This book is something of an industry first in the way it deals with this subject. We will explore techniques for managing stress and anxiety, and strategies for building resilience and coping with setbacks. My goal is to help you become the best version of yourself, both in your professional and personal life. By combining the latest research with real-world experience, I firmly believe this book will be an invaluable resource for anyone looking to achieve excellence in the aviation and aerospace industries or for those interested in pursuing careers in the field.

Our thinking patterns play a crucial role in achieving excellence. That is why this book places a great emphasis on the topic of better thinking. We delve into the different types of thinking that are necessary to excel in this field, including analytical, creative, and critical thinking. We also explore the common thinking traps and biases that can lead to poor decisions and performance and how to avoid folly, misjudgment and misguidance. Ultimately, the goal of this book is to provide aviation and aerospace professionals with the mental tools and strategies they need to achieve peak performance and excellence, while also promoting their overall well-being and mental health. By doing so, we can ensure that the future of the industry is in good hands, and that we continue to push the boundaries of what is possible in aviation and aerospace. As someone who has dedicated a lot of time and effort to the study and application of practical and positive psychology, I'm incredibly excited to be able to combine that passion with my love of aviation and aerospace. I truly believe that this book and course will help you to achieve excellence in your careers, and to strive to live fulfilling and meaningful lives. We all know that the world we live in can be incredibly challenging, with constant pressures and demands pulling us in different directions. If you are struggling with mental health issues, it is vital to seek assistance from your trained medical professional, doctor and to engage with qualified experts with evidence-based approaches to help you. This book is to help guide you and provide you with tools and options to assist you on your journey in wellbeing and should not be approached as a substitute to those resources, but rather as a supplement. With the right tools and techniques, we can all learn to be resilient in the face of adversity, and to perform at the highest standards of professionalism, excellence and safety. And that's exactly what this book is all about. I know that many of you have chosen careers in aviation and aerospace because you're passionate about making a difference in the field, about pushing the boundaries of what's possible, and about being part of this extraordinary and dynamic industry. I believe that this book will help you to do all those things and more and I'm honored to be able to play a small part in that journey.

Noel Cox

2023

SECTION 1

MENTAL TRAINING FOR EXCELLENCE

Building Resilience

As an aviation and aerospace professional, you are no stranger to the concept of resilience. Every day, you face challenges and obstacles that require you to adapt and overcome. Resilience is more than just bouncing back from setbacks and challenges. It's about having the inner strength and fortitude to persevere through difficult times and emerge stronger on the other side. I believe that building resilience is one of the most important things you can do for your personal and professional development. When you can weather the storms that inevitably come your way, you can stay focused and motivated on your goals, and ultimately achieve greater success.

Let's look at some innovative approaches that give you the tools and skills you need to care for your mental health and wellbeing and pursue personal and professional excellence. The unique set of ideas and concepts laid out in this work may be somewhat surprising to some of the readers, and the overall approach is quite different to anything else out there dealing with this subject, and therein lies the additional value. These approaches are based on decades of direct experience in the industry and a unique and pioneering blend of both ancient and modern evidence-based mental training methods to assist you to be the best you can be. I will teach you about new ways of thinking. Good thinking is increasingly more important in this modern society of social media and algorithms seeking to capture and influence your attention. It means being able to approach problems and challenges in new and innovative ways. It means being able to generate creative solutions and anticipate potential obstacles. All of this requires mental training, just like physical training is required to be at the top of your game physically. You need to exercise your mind, to develop new habits of thought and to break free of old patterns. You need to learn how to think creatively, to connect seemingly unrelated concepts and ideas in new and exciting ways. I will explain in this work why innovative thinking is so important in a dynamic ever-changing world. Developing a Top Mind is about mastering the art of thinking. In this work you will find a range of techniques and tools to help people break through mental barriers and unlock more of your creative potential. With this mental training system, you will improve your thinking skills and achieve excellence in all that you do. One of the biggest obstacles to good thinking is our tendency to get stuck in our own perspectives and beliefs. We can become so attached to our own ideas that we are unable to see other possibilities, and we end up missing out on valuable opportunities. This work will help you cultivate a mindset of curiosity and exploration. To be willing to challenge our own assumptions and limiting beliefs, and to consider alternative perspectives. This will require mental flexibility on your part and a willingness to step outside your comfort zone. Divergent thinking is another key component of good thinking, and it's a skill that you can learn to develop and practice. Essentially, divergent thinking is the ability to generate multiple ideas or solutions to a problem. Instead of settling on the first idea that comes to mind, divergent thinking involves exploring a wide range of possibilities and considering alternative perspectives. The key to divergent thinking is to approach problems with an open mind and a willingness to explore a wide range of possibilities. It's about breaking out of your usual patterns of thinking and considering new perspectives and approaches. This work itself is a result of divergent thinking, in that it draws from a range of disciplines to provide a holistic solution to wellbeing for your profession.

This book will help you to awaken the strength of the human spirit, which is something that cannot be measured by the size of our muscles or the depth of our pockets. It lies within each of us, waiting to be awakened.

The human spirit allows us to endure the greatest hardships, to face the most daunting challenges, and to overcome the most difficult obstacles. It is the strength that inspires us to fight for what is right, to stand up for our values and principles, and to never give up in the face of adversity. This strength does not come naturally to most of us. It must be developed and nurtured, like a seed that needs sunlight and water to grow. We must cultivate this strength within ourselves, through hard work, discipline, and a relentless commitment to the pursuit of personal and professional excellence. We achieve this by tapping into the power of our minds, by harnessing the energy of our thoughts and emotions, and channeling them towards positive action. We do it by training our minds to focus on our wellbeing and mental health, to stay calm and centered in the face of chaos, and to believe in our own abilities even when others doubt us. This is the strength of the human spirit that has fueled the greatest champions in history, from Olympic winners, Nobel Laureates, first responders saving lives and protecting us, to the astronauts that explore space. It is the strength of the human spirit that will carry us through the toughest times, and it is the strength that will ultimately lead us to excellence in our lives. How do we tap into this inner power that can move mountains and conquer the impossible? It starts with the mind. You see, the mind is a powerful tool that can either work for us or against us. If we allow our fears, doubts, and insecurities to control our thoughts, then we are limiting ourselves and our potential. Through the exercises in this course, we can learn to control our minds, to focus our thoughts on positivity, on growth, on possibility, then we can unlock the full strength of our spirit. With practice, with discipline, we can train our minds to work for us instead of against us. We can learn to quiet the noise and listen to the stillness within us, where our true strength lies. Your mind is a powerful tool, and the thoughts that you feed it can have a tremendous impact on your life. When you focus your mind on positive thoughts and outcomes, you attract positive energy and opportunities into your life. When you focus your mind on positive outcomes and opportunities, you open yourself up to new possibilities and attract success and achievement into your life. It's about shifting our mindset from one of doubt and negativity to one of confidence and possibility. It's a lifelong process of continuous improvement. You must continually feed your mind with positive thoughts and surround yourself with positive influences to maintain a positive mindset. We continue the journey along the path of excellence step by step.

"It is what it is!"

The approach of "It is what it is" is rooted in the notion of taking the world as it is presented to us. Rather than imposing our own subjective and often erroneous interpretations on a given set of circumstances, we choose instead to apprehend reality on its own terms, to discern the essential features of a given phenomenon, and to make our decisions accordingly. The strength of this approach lies in its steadfast commitment to empirical observation and the unvarnished truth. It challenges us to cast aside our preconceptions, biases, and prejudices, and to examine the facts of a situation with dispassionate objectivity. By doing so, we can avoid the pitfalls of wishful thinking and self-delusion and arrive at more accurate and effective strategies for navigating the world. The veracity of this approach must, of course, be subjected to rigorous scrutiny. We must continually test its validity and reliability and ensure that it withstands the test of time. We must also remain vigilant against the tendency to project our own desires and aspirations onto a given set of circumstances, and to always strive for a clear-eyed view of reality. In short, the "It is what it is" approach represents a bold and courageous attempt to grapple with the complexities of the world as it is, rather than as we might wish it to be. It is a call to intellectual honesty, to a steadfast commitment to the truth, and to the courage to face the world on its own terms. In your field, precision, accuracy, and attention to detail are paramount, and the decisions you make can have a profound impact on the safety and well-being of countless individuals. It is therefore essential that you approach each situation with a clear-eyed and objective perspective, free from the distortions of subjective interpretation and hasty assumptions.

By adopting an "It is what it is" approach, you can avoid the pitfalls of wishful thinking and self-delusion, and instead focus on the facts of the situation at hand. Whether you are facing a potential safety issue or a technical problem, you can rely on a rigorous analysis of empirical data and objective observations to arrive at the best possible course of action.

Furthermore, this approach can also be applied to the broader context of your life and your career. By remaining committed to objective observation and empirical data, you can avoid the pitfalls of self-deception and wishful thinking and make decisions that are grounded and based on a clear-eyed assessment of your own strengths, weaknesses, and goals. Remain steadfast in your commitment to the truth, to a rigorous analysis of the facts, and to an "It is what it is" approach that will enable you to navigate the complexities of your work with clarity, precision, and objectivity. By doing so, you will be able to make decisions that are grounded in reality and that lead to the best possible outcomes for yourselves, your colleagues, and your passengers.

Allow me to illustrate the importance of adopting an "It is what it is" approach with a simple example involving a pet python.

As you may know, some individuals keep pythons as pets, and in some cases, they mistakenly project their own human-like personality traits onto these animals. They may assume that their pet python is capable of feeling emotions or of exhibiting behaviors that are more commonly associated with human beings, when in fact the python is a uniquely snake-like creature, with its own distinct set of instincts and behaviors. This kind of projection can have serious consequences, both for the python and for its owner. If the owner assumes that their python is capable of behaving in a certain way, based on their own preconceived notions of what a pet "should" be like, they may unwittingly put themselves in harm's way. For example, they may assume that their pet python is "friendly" and can be handled in a certain way, when in fact the snake is simply following its own instincts and may attack if it feels threatened. The key to avoiding these kinds of misunderstandings is to adopt an "It is what it is" approach. By recognizing that the python is a uniquely snake-like creature, with its own set of behaviors and instincts, the owner can avoid projecting their own human-like personality traits onto the animal and can instead make decisions based on a clear-eyed and objective assessment of the python's actual behaviors and needs. Remain committed to the truth, to a rigorous analysis of the facts, and to an "It is what it is" approach in all aspects of your work and your life. By doing so, you can avoid the pitfalls of projection and self-deception, and make decisions that are grounded and that lead to the best possible outcomes for yourselves and those around you. I'm reminded of another related concept that has been observed in particularly resilient flight crews throughout the years. This concept involves their remarkable capacity to deal with unexpected delays and issues that can arise during flight operations. I've had the privilege of working with some of the most calm and competent crews and ground personnel, truly world class teams who have faced highly stressful situations such as delays and cancellations with a remarkable sense of equanimity and professionalism. Instead of allowing themselves to be consumed by frustration or anger, they have approached severe delays and other major inconveniences with a solution-oriented mindset, focusing on what needs to be done to get the flight back on track, rather than on the obstacles that stand in their way. At the heart of this mindset is the simple but profound concept that "It's a part of life." By recognizing that unexpected delays and other issues are an inevitable part of the flight operations, these crews have been able to avoid becoming frustrated and overwhelmed by the situation and have instead focused on the facts of the situation at hand and use their knowledge and experience to immediately set about solving the problem and getting underway. They also demonstrated a tremendous capacity to remain positive that the issue could be resolved in an efficient and effective a way as possible. This approach has allowed them to remain flexible and adaptable, and to make decisions that lead to the best possible outcomes for themselves and their passengers and colleagues alike. It has also allowed them to maintain a sense of calm and professionalism in the face of adversity, which has undoubtedly contributed to the safety and well-being of all those involved in the flight operations. Consider adopting this solution-oriented mindset in your own work and your own life, recognizing that unexpected delays and issues are an inevitable part of any complex system, and that the key to success lies in remaining focused on the facts of the situation. By doing so, we can remain flexible, adaptable, and resilient in the face of adversity, and can make decisions that lead to the best possible outcomes for ourselves and those around us.

On one occasion, a pilot I know was informed that his flight would be delayed due to a mechanical issue with the aircraft. As you can imagine, this news was not well received by the passengers or the crew, and tensions were running high.

Rather than allow himself to be consumed by frustration or anger, the pilot took a deep breath and reminded himself that delays are an inevitable part of the flight operations. He recognized that projecting his own expectations or desires onto the situation would only lead to further stress and frustration, and that the key to success lay in focusing on the facts of the situation at hand. The pilot immediately began to work with his crew and ground personnel to come up with a solution that would minimize the delay and get the flight back on track as quickly as possible. He remained calm and professional throughout the process, reassuring his passengers and keeping everyone informed of the situation. Through his leadership and his solution-oriented mindset, the pilot was able to turn a potentially chaotic situation into a smooth and well-managed operation. The delay was minimized, and the flight arrived at its destination only slightly behind schedule. As I have illustrated through my examples, adopting an "It is what it is" approach is closely related to the concept of perceptual reframing, which involves shifting our perspective and reframing our understanding of a situation. By doing so, we can often unlock new solutions and possibilities that were not previously apparent. In the case of the delayed flight, the pilot was able to reframe the situation by recognizing that delays are an inevitable part of the flight operations, rather than perceiving the situation as an inconvenience or a personal setback. This allowed him to approach the situation with a clearer and more solution-oriented mindset, leading to a better outcome for all involved. By recognizing and reframing our thoughts and perceptions, we can improve our emotional resilience, problem-solving abilities, and overall wellbeing. In your work unexpected delays and challenges are a common occurrence, adopting the "It is what it is" and "It's a part of life" approach can be a powerful tool for managing stress, building resilience, and achieving better outcomes. It allows us to approach challenges with a clear head and a solution-oriented mindset, rather than becoming consumed by frustration or anxiety.

Exercise

I would like to provide you with an exercise that demonstrates the effectiveness of the "It is what it is" approach and the power of perceptual reframing.

The exercise is simple and can be done in just a few minutes. Find a quiet and comfortable space where you will not be disturbed and take a few deep breaths to center yourself.

Next, think of a recent situation in your life where you encountered a challenge or setback. It could be a work-related issue, a personal conflict, or anything that caused you stress or frustration.

Once you have identified this situation, take a moment to reframe it using the "It is what it is" approach. Ask yourself: "What are the facts of this situation, and what can I do to move forward from here?"

Focus on the objective facts of the situation, rather than your own projections or emotions. Ask yourself: "What opportunities or solutions are available to me now, and how can I approach this situation with a solution-oriented mindset?"

By reframing the situation in this way, you may find that new solutions and possibilities emerge that were not previously apparent. You may also find that your stress and frustration dissipate as you focus on the facts of the situation and the solutions available to you.

I would like to share with you some questions that can help you transition into a solution-oriented mindset when facing challenges or setbacks. These questions are designed to help you focus on the objective facts of the situation and identify opportunities and solutions that may not be immediately apparent. By asking these questions, you can shift your perspective from one of frustration or helplessness to one of empowerment and creativity.

Here are some of the best questions to ask yourself when facing a challenge or setback.

What are the facts of this situation?

What are the possible solutions or opportunities that I may be overlooking?

What resources or support do I have available to me?

What can I do right now to make progress or move towards a solution?

What can I learn from this situation that will help me in the future?

Asking these questions can help you approach challenges and setbacks with a clear and focused mind and can help you identify creative solutions that may have otherwise gone unnoticed.

The traits of resilience were captured in a review by (Ropp, T., Belt S., 2020)

"...With the goal of developing observable, behavioral-based actions that could be incorporated into pedagogical or anagogical applications, five prominent resilience trait categories with subsequent behavioral descriptions were identified:

1. Adversity persistence (adaptability and perseverance), 2. Contextual awareness (picture making; visualizing and assessing problems and synthesizing decision strategies) 3. Self-directed action/ learning autonomy, 4. Change Management and Innovation during initial failure or difficulty, 5. Social connectivity (peer relationships)..."[2]

Pilots face unexpected situations all the time, and the ability to adapt and persevere through adversity is crucial. It's essential to have a strong situational awareness, to understand the context of the situation, and to make decisions based on that understanding. By practicing these skills, you can make better decisions and avoid errors. You need to be self-motivated and take responsibility for your own learning and development. When something goes wrong, you need to be able to think creatively and adapt your approach. Aviation is a team sport, and pilots rely on one another for support and collaboration. By cultivating strong relationships with your colleagues, you can improve communication, build trust, and create a more effective team.

Mental Toughness and Focus

Let's examine some of the strategies that can help you excel in high performance work scenarios and the practical application of mental toughness and focus in the workplace. Mental toughness is the ability to stay calm, focused, and resilient in the face of adversity. It's the quality that allows you to persevere and push through challenging situations. One of the keys to developing mental toughness is to reframe challenges as opportunities for growth. Some people whom I worked with when faced with particularly challenging performance situations would relish it, they would love a tough crosswind landing or difficult challenges and one of my colleagues used to repeat, "It's an opportunity to shine buddy." Instead of being intimidated by obstacles, use them as a chance to learn and improve, to rise to the challenge and enjoy the degree of difficulty. Mental toughness is not just about being able to handle tough situations, it's about being able to push through when things get really hard. One of the key things that has helped me is developing a habit of discipline. When you have a habit of discipline, you can push through anything. You need to have a routine and stick to it. When things get tough, you must embrace the opportunity to shine and keep pushing. You also need to focus on what you can control. There are a lot of things in life that are outside of our control, but we can control our attitude and our effort. Physical fitness is a huge part of developing mental toughness. When you're pushing yourself physically, you're also pushing yourself mentally. You realize that you can do more than you ever thought possible. It's also a great way to build discipline and develop a routine. When things get hard, you can either shy away from it or lean into it. That's where real growth happens. Believe that you can get better, that you can learn from your failures and mistakes. That's how you turn adversity into an opportunity. When you can see yourself succeeding, when you can feel it in your bones, that's when you start to make it a reality. It's about creating a mental image of the person you want to be and then working every day to become that person. Mental toughness isn't something that comes easy, you must earn it. It's about being consistent and showing up every day, no matter how you feel. Mental toughness isn't a destination, it's a journey. It's something you may cultivate every day. The more you work at it, the stronger you become. It's not about being perfect, it's about progress. As long as you're moving forward, you're on the right track. setbacks are just temporary. Keep pushing and stay focused on your goals. If you fail, use it as a learning opportunity and come back even stronger. Have a clear sense of purpose and direction in life. When you have a strong "why," you're much more likely to stay committed and motivated, even when things get tough. Take action and put in the work to make your goals a reality. That's where discipline comes in. Discipline is the foundation of mental toughness. Discipline is a muscle that you need to train just like any other muscle. Push yourself out of your comfort zone and challenge yourself to do things you don't want to do. You can't blame anyone else for your situation or your problems. Take responsibility for your life and your choices. That's the only way you can truly take control and create the life you want. It's not just about what you say to yourself, it's also about how you carry yourself. Stand up straight, shoulders back, head held high. It's a small thing, but it can make a big difference in how you feel and how others perceive you. Instead of viewing failures or setbacks as obstacles, pilots should see them as opportunities for growth and improvement. For example, if a pilot makes a mistake during a flight, instead of beating themselves up over it, they can use it as a learning experience to improve their skills and become a better pilot. You should aim to maintain a healthy lifestyle, exercise regularly, and get enough sleep. This not only helps to improve their physical health but also their mental resilience and ability to handle stress in the air. Focus is a critical component. It's the ability to concentrate on the task at hand and avoid distractions. Instead of dwelling on things that are out of your control, focus on acting on the things you can control. Research undertaken by Bor et al. (2017) indicates that certain psychological problems in pilots include anxiety and occupational stress, relationship problems, and even alcohol problems.[3]

Regular exercise can help reduce stress and improve cognitive function, while a healthy diet and sufficient sleep can improve mood and concentration.

By reframing challenges as opportunities, practicing mindfulness meditation, cultivating a positive mindset, and taking care of your physical health, you can develop these qualities and achieve peak performance. Mental toughness is not something you're born with; it's a skill that can be learned and developed with practice. It's less about being the right stuff, but more about doing the right stuff. Part of mental toughness training is developing the skills of cognitive flexibility, or the ability to switch between different tasks and adapt to changing conditions. Research by (Sung et al., 2019) indicated that "*..Stress is closely associated with not only physical illness but also with indices of psychological maladjustment. However, such negative mental health outcomes may vary depending on the individual's cognitive style, or perception of stress. Air force pilots are particularly vulnerable to experience a high degree of stress as they are required to conduct missions while simultaneously monitoring for safety in complex and uncertain flight situations. It can thus be posited that appropriate use of cognitive stress management strategies is one of the crucial competency requirements for pilots..*"*[4]*

Cognitive stress management and flexibility are very important for developing resilience. Here are some innovative ways to develop cognitive flexibility. Flight situations are often unpredictable and uncertain, and pilots must learn to adapt to these situations quickly. Pilots can develop cognitive flexibility by embracing uncertainty and learning to approach problems with a more open-minded and flexible attitude. Learn and practice doing things in new ways. Change things up, move your furniture around, try adopting feng shui principles in your home, take different routes, be creative. Try out new sports and interests.

Role-playing exercises in training can be an effective way to practice cognitive flexibility. This involves taking on the perspective of someone else and seeing the world from their point of view. This helps to develop empathy and the ability to see things from multiple perspectives. The military are particularly good at creating exercises that put cadets and trainees out of their comfort zones and into scenarios that require them to adapt. Initiative is highly valued in these cases.

Engaging in creative problem-solving exercises can help to develop cognitive flexibility by encouraging individuals to think outside the box and consider alternative solutions to a problem. This can include brainstorming sessions, ideation exercises, and other creative thinking techniques.

Cross-training involves learning new skills or taking on new roles within an organization. This can help to develop cognitive flexibility by exposing individuals to new challenges and situations that require them to adapt and learn new ways of thinking.

Experiential learning involves learning by doing. This approach can help to develop cognitive flexibility by allowing individuals to learn from their mistakes and adapt their thinking based on the outcomes of their actions. Self-directed action and learning autonomy are essential for continuous improvement and growth. Pilots who take ownership of their own learning and development can build the skills and knowledge needed to excel in their careers.

Mind mapping is a visual thinking tool that involves creating a diagram of ideas and concepts. This technique can help to develop cognitive flexibility by encouraging individuals to make connections between different ideas and consider alternative ways of organizing information.

Language learning and trying new cultural things can even help with cognitive flexibility. New skills such as martial arts are great for this, as they engage that mind and body link in new and interesting ways. By engaging in these innovative approaches, individuals can learn to adapt to new situations, think creatively, and approach challenges with an open mind. That's why life experiences are great at teaching us to adapt to alternative approaches to things. I have always had a passion for travel and while travelling the world, I loved learning the way different people and cultures do things and was often astonished to find much better ways of doing things in the most unexpected places.

Focus During Training.

When you enter your training focus, it's essential to have a detailed plan for each session and each mission. Planning helps you stay focused and avoid distractions. For example, have a written plan for each day that includes specific goals, workouts, and recovery activities. Keep a detailed log of your progress and any challenges you encounter, so you can analyze them and adjust my plan accordingly. Planning is not enough. You also need to be able to evaluate your performance objectively and learn from your mistakes. I recommend keeping a detailed journal or a voice recorder to document your thoughts and emotions before, during, and after each training session for an upcoming performance. This will help you identify patterns and areas where you need to improve. A crucial aspect of mental training is the ability to focus your mind and control your thoughts. One technique that you should practice is to visualize the perfect flight, step by step, in your mind. You would imagine every detail, from pre-flight preparation to the checklists and briefings, and how you will overcome any obstacles that might arise and go around procedures and alternative airports. Visualization helps to program your mind and increase your confidence and resilience. When you encounter setbacks or failures in your training, see them as opportunities to learn and grow, rather than as obstacles that define your worth.

Plan, Prepare, and Execute. Ready, Aim, Fire!

To excel in aviation, you need a plan, prepare well and execute your plans with precision. Plan your flight and fly your plan. Mental training takes time, patience, and discipline to master.

The first step is to identify your objective, whether it's completing a successful flight in the most resourceful state of mind you can, achieving a certain performance metric, or simply wanting to be the best aviator you can possibly be. Once you have identified your key objectives, it's essential to break them down into smaller, more manageable objectives. This could include things like flight planning, pre-flight checks, weather analysis, and communication with your team.

The next step is preparation. This involves taking the necessary steps to ensure that you are fully mentally prepared for your performance and attain the correct focus and empowering state of mind to show up at your best and ready to achieve your personal and professional objectives. It's also important to consider potential personal challenges or obstacles that may arise during the flight and have contingency plans in place for how you will maintain your composure and deal with them.

Then there is execution. This is where all your planning and preparation come together, and you put your training and expertise into action. It's essential to stay focused, alert, and aware of your surroundings, and to adjust as necessary to ensure you perform at your best.

In aviation, as in sports, continuous improvement is key to long-term success. This means regularly reviewing your performance and evaluating your progress towards your goals. One effective way to do this is through self-reflection and analysis, using tools like post-flight debriefs and performance metrics on yourself. This allows you to identify areas where you can improve and adjust your own mental training and development plan and preparation accordingly.

The evaluations can be as simple as answering the following questions in detail,

What went well?

What did not go as well as expected?

What can I do better next time?

By answering these questions in detailed written form, you are focused on results, you are using a kind of cybernetic feedback loop of information that you can adopt and continually improve. It's like the guidance system on a spacecraft, constantly monitoring the trajectory and parameters and adjusting along the way so that you can reach your destination. Excellence in short is about constant discipline and persistent effort at improving and planning, preparation, and execution are the building blocks of success in any field, and aviation is no exception.

Modes of Thinking

In this section I want to provide you with some useful insights and tools that can help us think more critically, rationally, and effectively.

Let's start by acknowledging that we are all prone to cognitive biases and errors. These biases are systematic deviations from rationality that affect our judgment and decision-making. Some of the most common biases include the confirmation bias, which leads us to seek and interpret information that confirms our preexisting beliefs, the availability bias, which makes us overestimate the likelihood of events that are more memorable or vivid, and the framing effect, which shows that our choices are influenced by how the options are presented to us.

How can we overcome these biases and improve our thinking? One way is to cultivate what Daniel Kahneman calls a "slow thinking" mode, which is characterized by deliberate and reflective processing of information. This mode involves paying attention to details, questioning assumptions, and considering alternative explanations. It is the opposite of what he calls "fast thinking," which relies on automatic and intuitive judgments based on heuristics and emotions.

Another tool that can help us think more critically is the use of decision-making frameworks. These frameworks provide a structured way of analyzing complex problems and making decisions based on explicit criteria. One example of such a framework is the "pros and cons" list which we mentioned earlier in reference to the Benjamin Franklin method, which involves weighing the advantages and disadvantages of a given option. Another example is the decision tree, which involves mapping out the possible outcomes of different choices and their probabilities.

Let's consider how we can apply these insights and tools to real-life situations. For example, let's say you are considering investing in a new business venture. Your fast thinking mode might tell you that the opportunity is too good to pass up, based on some anecdotal evidence or a persuasive pitch. However, if you activate your slow thinking mode and use a decision-making framework, you might uncover some red flags or uncertainties that were overlooked. You might consider the risks and rewards more carefully and seek out more information before making a final decision.

In another example, let's say you are trying to resolve a conflict with a colleague or family member. Your fast thinking mode might lead you to become defensive or emotional, and to focus on winning the argument rather than finding a mutually satisfactory solution. However, if you activate your slow thinking mode and use some communication skills, you might listen actively to the other person's perspective, express your own feelings and needs clearly, and seek common ground. You might find that by reframing the problem or exploring creative options, you can reach a more productive outcome.

Improving our thinking is a lifelong endeavor that requires self-awareness, practice, and discipline. By recognizing our cognitive biases and limitations, and by cultivating a slow thinking mode and using decision-making frameworks, we can make better choices and solve problems more effectively.

Consider the role of automation in aviation. Modern aircraft are equipped with advanced automation systems that can assist pilots in various aspects of their duties, from navigation to communication and even decision-making. However, it's important to recognize that automation can also introduce new sources of error and complexity, especially if pilots don't fully understand how the systems work and rely too much on them.

To avoid this, it's essential that pilots receive thorough training on how to operate and monitor the automation systems, as well as on how to recognize and manage situations where the systems may not be functioning as expected. Additionally, it's important for pilots to maintain a high level of situational awareness and to continuously monitor their own performance and decision-making processes, so they can detect and correct errors before they escalate into more serious issues.

Another important application of these insights is in the area of crew resource management (CRM). Aviation is a highly collaborative activity that involves many different individuals with different roles and responsibilities. Effective CRM requires that all members of the crew communicate effectively, share information, and work together to make decisions that promote safety and efficiency.

To achieve this, crew members are trained in effective communication and decision-making skills, as well as in strategies for managing conflict and resolving disagreements. Crew members need to recognize and manage cognitive biases that can affect their own thinking and decision-making processes, as well as those of their colleagues. A safety culture refers to the attitudes, values, and practices that govern how safety is prioritized and managed within an organization. A strong safety culture is essential for promoting safety and reducing the risk of accidents and incidents.

This means organizations need to recognize and address cognitive biases that can affect safety culture, such as complacency, normalization of deviance, and overconfidence. Organizations should foster cultures of continuous learning and improvement, where all members are encouraged to report safety incidents and near-misses, and to participate in regular safety training and drills. By understanding how our minds work and how cognitive biases can affect our performance, pilots and other aviation professionals can take steps to improve their decision-making, enhance crew resource management, and promote a strong safety culture.

Lateral Thinking

Lateral thinking is the process of approaching a problem or idea from a completely different perspective, rather than just trying to solve it by using traditional methods. It encourages you to think outside the box and consider alternative solutions that may not have been immediately obvious. For example, imagine that you are an aerospace design engineer trying to solve a problem regarding a flight engine. Instead of just focusing on the immediate issue, use lateral thinking to consider how the problem might be solved in a completely different way. Could the issue be solved by changing the way the engine is designed, or by using different materials in its construction? By asking these types of questions, you may be able to come up with a more effective solution that you would not have otherwise considered. Another method that can be applied is the use of "random input." This involves taking a seemingly unrelated object or idea and using it as inspiration for solving a problem. For example, you may be struggling with finding a solution to a problem in cockpit design. By using a completely unrelated object or idea, such as a tree, you may be able to generate new ideas and solutions that you may not have considered otherwise.

Mind mapping is a useful visual tool that can help you organize and structure your thoughts and ideas in a non-linear way. It can be particularly helpful when trying to solve complex problems or generate new ideas. For example, you could create a mind map of all the different components of an airplane and their functions, and then use this to identify potential areas for improvement or optimization.

For example, if you are experiencing an issue with the plane's design for specific and perhaps unusual operating environments, you could use the word "inverted" as a random entry. This may seem unrelated at first, but it could inspire you to think about solutions that involve using inverted lift design to slow down, create drag or loose height in an efficient manner with a change of configuration of a device that can be redesigned with new capabilities on the aircraft. These may seem like far-fetched solutions, but they could lead to innovative ideas that could potentially solve the problem. By using these methods, you can come up with innovative solutions that could improve safety, efficiency, and the passenger experience. Approach problems with an open mind, and don't be afraid to explore unconventional solutions.

Better Thinking by Avoiding Folly, Misjudgment and Misguidance.

In the world of aviation and aerospace it is crucial to develop a clear understanding of the cognitive biases and heuristics that can lead to poor decision-making. Take a multidisciplinary approach to problem-solving. This means bringing together experts from a variety of fields to analyze the issue from different perspectives and identify potential blind spots. It also means being willing to challenge your own assumptions and seek out diverse viewpoints. rationality and clear thinking. Emotions and biases can cloud our judgment and lead to poor decisions. Therefore, it is crucial to approach problems with a clear mind and to use data and facts to inform your decision-making process. In aviation and aerospace, where precision is crucial, it is especially important to avoid snap judgments or emotional responses. The avoidance of folly in thinking is not simply about avoiding big, catastrophic mistakes, but rather about consistently making wise decisions and avoiding errors, both large and small. And the best way to do this is to understand the principles of human psychology and behavior and use them to your advantage. People are motivated by incentives, whether they be financial, social, or psychological. In the aviation and aerospace industries, the incentives can range from executive bonuses for on-time departures to reputational gains for successful missions. However, these incentives can also create misalignments, leading people to make decisions that are not in the best interests of the company or their customers. To avoid this, it is important to cultivate a culture of transparency and accountability. This means creating an environment where people are encouraged to speak up when they see potential problems or risks, and where leaders are held accountable for the decisions they make. By doing so, we can avoid the kinds of misjudgments and misguidance that can lead to serious consequences. Another key principle is the importance of diversity of thought. In the aviation and aerospace industries, we rely on teams of experts to make critical decisions. But if everyone on the team thinks the same way, we risk missing important perspectives and potential solutions. By embracing diversity of thought and encouraging people to bring their unique perspectives to the table, we can make better decisions and avoid the kind of groupthink that can lead to errors of judgment. Leadership needs to learn humility. No matter how much expertise or experience we have, we are all fallible human beings capable of making mistakes. By recognizing our limitations and being open to feedback and learning, we can continue to grow and improve, both as leaders and as a team. Avoiding folly in thinking and misjudgments requires a conscious effort to identify and correct our own biases and blind spots. We all have inherent biases and mental models that shape our thinking, but it's important to recognize them and challenge them when necessary. You can also engineer your thinking by inverting the process. Instead of focusing only on what you should do to achieve success, you can also consider what we should avoid doing to prevent failure. By thinking in this way, you and your teams can identify potential pitfalls and blind spots that we might otherwise overlook, especially in aircraft and spacecraft design. Understand what you are good at and recognize the boundaries or sphere of your competence. This refers to the idea that we should focus on what we know and understand and be very diligent when venturing into areas where we lack expertise. By staying within our sphere of competence, we can make more informed decisions and avoid costly mistakes. In addition to avoiding folly in thinking and misjudgments, it's important to also be mindful of misguidance. This can come from external sources such as media, peer pressure, or groupthink, and can lead us down the wrong path. To combat misguidance, we must be willing to think independently and critically evaluate information before accepting it as truth. We must also surround ourselves with people who encourage us to think independently and challenge our assumptions, rather than those who simply echo our own beliefs. I've seen some people make some foolish decisions in my time. I've seen people make impulsive choices, driven by emotion or ego, and it invariably leads to trouble. On the other had I've also seen people who have exercised good judgment, who have taken a step back and thought things through carefully, and they've achieved incredible success.

Always think critically. Always question your assumptions, always seek out new information, and always be willing to change your mind when the evidence warrants it. Don't be afraid to ask for help or seek out the opinions of others, but also be willing to stand firm in your convictions when you know you're right.

The best way to avoid folly in thinking is to be constantly learning and growing. Read widely and deeply, seek out new experiences and challenges, and always strive to be better tomorrow than you are today.

You all have a particular expertise and skill set that is crucial for your work. However, expertise alone is not enough for wise judgment. You must also be well-versed in other relevant areas, such as risk management, decision-making, and even philosophy. Be aware of your own biases and limitations. We all have them, whether we like to admit it or not. The key is to acknowledge them and actively work to overcome them.

You can start by seeking out information and opinions that challenge our own. It's easy to surround ourselves with people who think like us, but that can lead to a dangerous echo chamber. We must expose ourselves to diverse perspectives and be willing to consider them with an open mind.

Wise judgment and avoiding being misguided require a multidisciplinary approach and an awareness of our own biases. It takes effort and humility to achieve, but the rewards are immeasurable. Another crucial aspect of wise judgment is being able to recognize and avoid the common pitfalls of the human mind. We all have biases and heuristics that can lead us astray, and it's important to be aware of them so that we can compensate for them. This is why I encourage everyone to learn about cognitive biases and how they can impact decision-making. I recommend reading Charlie Munger's talks on these areas as they are very insightful. The key to making wise judgments is to have the right mindset. You need to be open-minded, curious, and willing to consider multiple perspectives. You need to be humble enough to admit when you're wrong and have the courage to change course when necessary. A first officer must have the confidence to question and provide feedback to a captain if he thinks what he is doing is wrong and the captain much take this into account. The same with commanders on space missions, crew chiefs on the ground, loading supervisors, or ATC supervisors, all of them can benefit from these principles.

A common thinking pitfall is confirmation bias, where you only seek out information that confirms our existing beliefs and ignore anything that contradicts them.

Another pitfall is the illusion of control, where we believe we have more control over a situation than we do. This can lead to overconfidence and poor decision-making and related to that is the sunk cost fallacy, where we continue to invest time, money, or other resources into a project or decision because we feel like we've already invested so much, even if it's not rational to do so.

One that also comes to mind is the availability heuristic, where we make decisions based on the most easily accessible information in our minds, rather than considering all relevant information. This can lead to inaccurate judgments and decisions and then there's also the bandwagon effect, where we make decisions or adopt beliefs because it's what everyone else is doing, rather than thinking critically about it ourselves.

Also, the framing effect, where the way a decision or question is presented can heavily influence our response, even if the underlying information is the same. It's amazing how many ways our minds can be misled. Staying aware of these common pitfalls, permits us to work to overcome them and make more rational, sound decisions. It's not just about avoiding mistakes, but also about creating opportunities for success. By understanding how our minds work and being more intentional about our decision-making, we can achieve greater outcomes in our personal and professional lives.

We all tend to rely on heuristics, or mental shortcuts, to make decisions. These heuristics can often lead us astray and cause us to make bad judgments.

Heuristics are often based on biases that are hardwired into our brains, and they can lead us to overlook important information or make snap judgments without thinking things through. Be consciously aware these biases exist and to actively work to counteract them by seeking out and considering alternative viewpoints, even if they contradict our own beliefs. By actively seeking out alternative viewpoints, we can gain a more well-rounded understanding of a situation and make more informed decisions.

In today's world, we're bombarded with so much information that it can be hard to distinguish between what's true and what's not. That's why it's so important to be a critical thinker and to always fact-check before making important decisions. It's so important to develop mental models and frameworks that can help guide our decision-making processes. By doing so, we can make better decisions and avoid the pitfalls of the human mind. None of us are immune to these pitfalls. It's a constant effort to remain vigilant and to keep improving our decision-making skills. By using mental models, you can get better outcomes. Mental models are simplified representations of reality that can be used to guide thinking and decision-making processes. They are like a map that helps us navigate complex situations, allowing us to make more informed choices and by having a framework to guide our decisions, we can minimize the impact of cognitive biases and prevent ourselves from falling into irrational thinking patterns.

Let's try a little aviation psychology game, shall we? I want you to imagine that you are piloting an aircraft in a difficult situation. You're feeling anxious, your heart rate is elevated, and you're struggling to keep your thoughts focused. What do you do?

Well, a technique that can be helpful in these situations is called box breathing. It's a simple but powerful way to control your breathing and calm your mind."

It works as follows, inhale slowly for a count of four, holding your breath for a count of four, exhaling slowly for a count of four, and then holding your breath again for a count of four. See how that feels? It's a great way to calm your mind and bring your focus back to the present moment.

He goes on to explain how this technique can be used not only in aviation but also in any situation, whether it's a business presentation or a sports match. It's all about controlling your mind and staying focused on the task at hand and with a little bit of practice, it becomes second nature.

Step onto the Flight Deck Confidently.

For new cadets and pilots, it may take a while to develop a sense of comfort and confidence going on the flight deck on a new type. Here is a psychological technique with you in mind. Think about a time when you were feeling confident, really on top of your game. Perhaps it was after a particularly successful project or after receiving some well-deserved recognition for your hard work. Now, as you think about that moment, notice how your body feels.

Do you feel taller, more upright, more energized?

Do you feel a sense of warmth or excitement in your chest?

Now, hold onto that feeling for a moment. And as you do, I'm going to suggest something to you. I want you to imagine that every time you step into a cockpit, you are stepping into that confident, successful moment. Rehearse and simulate that in your imagination. Imagine that every time you take control of the plane, you feel that same sense of energy and excitement that you felt before. Imbue it with as much detail as possible, imagine it in as close a detail as flight conditions as you can. Here's the thing, it doesn't matter if you're feeling nervous or unsure before you step into the cockpit you can learn to switch focus. All that matters is that you allow yourself to access that feeling of confidence and success. When you do, you'll be amazed at how much easier you can settle in and start to feel comfortable in the role.

Thought Labelling Principle

I'd like to share some of my thoughts and experiences with you on the topic of maintaining calm competence in operations and missions.

Aviation and aerospace can be dynamic industries, with complex and challenging situations that require quick thinking and sound decision-making. And yet, we know that the more stressed and anxious we become, the harder it is to think clearly and perform at our best.

What can we do to stay calm, cool, and collected in the face of such pressures?

I believe there are several key principles we can apply, drawn from the field of psychology. Recognize that our thoughts and emotions are not necessarily an accurate reflection of reality. Our brains are constantly interpreting and filtering information based on our past experiences, biases, and beliefs. When we're under pressure, those filters can become even more distorted. However, with practice, we can learn to observe our thoughts and emotions without getting swept away by them. One technique I like to use is what I call "thought labeling". When you notice yourself getting anxious or worried, simply label that thought or emotion as "anxiety" or "worry". This can help create some distance between you and the thought and make it easier to let it go. You can even discuss with yourself, "that is me feeling angry, and embarrassed. So that is how that feels." Somehow the phrasing of that can separate us from the intensity of the emotion and allow us to step back into the role of the calm observer rather than the experiencer.

First Principles Thinking

First Principles Thinking is a powerful approach to problem-solving that can help you achieve breakthroughs in your job and personal life. It's based on the idea of breaking down a problem or challenge into its fundamental elements or principles, and then re-building it from the ground up, rather than relying on assumptions or preconceived notions. This approach has been used by some of the most innovative and successful thinkers and companies, including Elon Musk and SpaceX, who have it to create revolutionary breakthroughs in the aerospace industry.

How can you apply this approach to your own life and work?

First, start by breaking down a problem or challenge into its most basic components or principles. Ask yourself: What are the core elements that make up this problem?

Next, challenge any assumptions or preconceived notions that you may have about the problem. Ask yourself, what do I truly know to be true about this problem, and what assumptions am I making that may be limiting my thinking?

Then, begin to re-build the problem from the ground up, using the fundamental principles that you have identified. Ask yourself: What are the most fundamental solutions to this problem, and how can I build upon these principles to create something truly innovative and effective?

By using First Principles Thinking, you can unlock new levels of creativity and problem-solving that you may not have thought possible. This approach can help you achieve breakthroughs in your work, your personal life, and any other area where you face challenges and obstacles.

Here are some real-life applications of First Principles Thinking in the aerospace industry.

Elon Musk's SpaceX used First Principles Thinking to revolutionize the rocket industry by developing reusable rockets. Instead of assuming that rockets had to be built as disposable, one-time-use vehicles, SpaceX broke down the problem and identified the core principles that make a rocket function. They then used these principles to re-build the rocket from the ground up, creating a design that allows the rocket to be re-used multiple times, significantly reducing the cost of space travel.

Boeing used this kind of thinking to create the B787 Dreamliner, a revolutionary new aircraft that is lighter, more fuel-efficient, and more comfortable for passengers. Boeing identified the core principles of aircraft design and challenged the assumption that planes had to be built with traditional materials like aluminum. They instead used cutting-edge composite materials to build the B787 Dreamliner, resulting in an aircraft that is significantly more efficient and comfortable than traditional planes.

NASA is currently using First Principles Thinking to plan its mission to Mars. By breaking down the problem of space travel to Mars into its most basic components, NASA can identify new solutions and approaches that were not previously considered. For example, NASA is exploring the use of 3D printing to create habitats on Mars, which would significantly reduce the cost and complexity of building structures on the planet.

These are just a few examples of how First Principles Thinking has been used in the aerospace industry to achieve breakthroughs and solve complex problems. However, the potential for creative applications of this approach is virtually limitless. By breaking down problems into their fundamental elements and challenging assumptions, individuals and organizations in any industry can unlock new levels of creativity and innovation.

Using First Principles Thinking you can identify the core problem of jet lag - the disruption of the body's circadian rhythm due to changes in light exposure and activity levels. With this understanding, one can then explore new solutions to address the root cause of the issue.

For example, an alternative approach to combat jet lag would be to adjust one's sleep schedule prior to the trip, gradually shifting the body's circadian rhythm to align with the destination time zone. This can be achieved by gradually adjusting the timing of sleep and light exposure over several days leading up to the flights.

One can make use of light therapy devices to simulate natural light exposure and help adjust the body's circadian rhythm. Engaging in physical activity and exercise during the day can also help regulate the body's internal clock and improve sleep quality.

The following is an example of a model for applying First Principles Thinking to any problem or issue.

Identify the problem or issue. Start by defining the problem or issue clearly and concisely. Be specific about what you are trying to solve or achieve.

Break the problem down into its fundamental elements, or first principles. This involves questioning and challenging assumptions and breaking down complex issues into simpler components. Gather data and evidence to support your understanding of the problem and the fundamental elements that make it up. This may involve research, experimentation, or consultation with experts. Analyze the data and evidence to identify patterns, relationships, and potential solutions. Look for opportunities to apply creative thinking and generate new ideas.

Based on the fundamental elements and the analysis of the data and evidence, build a new solution from the ground up. This may involve developing new processes or systems that challenge the status quo. Test the new solution in real-world scenarios and refine it based on feedback and results. Continuously improve and iterate the solution based on new information and insights. By following this model, you can apply it to any problem or issue, regardless of its complexity or scope. This approach encourages you to challenge assumptions, break down complex issues into simpler components, and build new solutions from the ground up, leading to more effective and innovative solutions.

Systems Thinking

Systems thinking involves looking at the big picture and considering all the different factors that contribute to a problem or situation. Systems thinking is a holistic approach to problem-solving that considers the interconnections and interdependencies among various components of a system. By applying this approach, you can identify the root causes of problems and find effective solutions that address the underlying issues. A practical way to apply systems thinking to your personal life is to focus on your overall well-being. Your well-being is influenced by various interconnected factors, such as your physical health, mental health, relationships, and environment. By examining how these factors are interconnected and interdependent, you can identify areas for improvement and make meaningful changes to enhance your well-being. For example, suppose you are experiencing stress and burnout at work. In that case, instead of simply addressing the symptoms of stress, such as sleeplessness or headaches, consider how your work environment, workload, and relationships with colleagues may be contributing to your stress. By identifying the root causes of your stress, you can develop effective solutions that address the underlying issues and promote your overall well-being.

Another practical application of systems thinking is to consider the impact of your actions on the environment. By examining the interconnections between your daily choices and their impact on the environment, you can identify ways to reduce your ecological footprint and promote sustainability. For example, you could reduce your energy consumption by using energy-efficient appliances or carpooling to work to reduce your carbon footprint. Whether you are addressing workplace stress, improving your overall well-being, or promoting sustainability, systems thinking can help you achieve your goals and improve your life.

As we have discussed, the systems thinking approach is useful for problem-solving and decision-making. In environments such as aviation and aerospace operations, it becomes even more critical to apply this approach effectively.

To apply the systems thinking approach in such dynamic environments, I recommend the following framework.

1. The first step is to identify the system or the problem you are trying to solve. The system can be flight operations, a maintenance process, mission control, air traffic control or any other aspect of the industry.
2. Once you have identified the system, the next step is to understand the interconnections between the different components of the system. This can include understanding how different departments and teams work together to ensure safe and efficient operations.
3. Feedback loops are an essential aspect of any system. They can be positive or negative and can have a significant impact on the performance of the system. Feedback loops are in the communication channels between different teams and departments.
4. Leverage points are areas where a small change can have a significant impact on the performance of the system. Leverage points can be found in the training and development of personnel, the implementation of new technologies, and the optimization of processes.
5. Act. Based on the analysis of the system, its interconnections, feedback loops, and leverage points, take action to improve the performance of the system. This includes implementing new processes, investing in technology, or improving communication channels between different teams and departments.

This framework helps you apply the systems thinking approach effectively in any of the high-pressure environments you may find yourself. Remember, a holistic understanding of the system and its interconnections can help you identify the most effective solutions and leverage points for improvement.

Examples of Practical Application

In air traffic control, the systems thinking approach can be particularly useful for improving the efficiency and safety of operations. The following framework can be applied:

1. Identify the goal of the system. The primary goal of air traffic control is to ensure the safe and efficient movement of aircraft.
2. Identify the system components. The key components of air traffic control include the aircraft, air traffic controllers, communication systems, weather monitoring systems, and airport infrastructure.
3. Identify the system interconnections. The interconnections between the system components are crucial to its overall performance. For example, the communication systems must be reliable and efficient to ensure effective coordination between air traffic controllers and pilots.
4. Identify the system feedback loops. Feedback loops are essential for maintaining the stability and resilience of the system. For example, if an aircraft encounters severe turbulence, air traffic controllers can provide feedback to other aircraft in the area to avoid the same turbulence.
5. Analyze the system behavior. By analyzing the behavior of the system, including potential failure modes and their consequences, air traffic controllers can identify areas for improvement and develop effective risk management strategies.
6. Develop interventions and monitor their effectiveness. Based on the analysis, interventions can be implemented to improve the performance of the system. For example, new communication protocols or technology can be introduced to enhance the efficiency of air traffic control. It is important

to monitor the effectiveness of these interventions and adjust them as needed.

Creative Thinking and Brainstorming

SCAMPER

SCAMPER is an acronym that stands for Substitute, Combine, Adapt, Modify, Put to another use, Eliminate, and Reverse. This technique is a tool for generating new ideas and exploring new possibilities.

Let's take a closer look,

Substitute. This is the idea of substituting one element of a product or process with another. For example, you might ask "What if we used a different material to construct the aircraft's frame?"

Combine. This looks at combining two or more elements of a product or process to create something new. For example, you might ask "What if we combined the design of a helicopter with that of an airplane?"

Adapt. This is modifying an existing product or process to make it work better for a different purpose. For example, you might ask "How can we adapt technology to improve air traffic control?"

Modify. This is about making small modifications to an existing product or process to improve it. For example, you might ask "How can we modify the design of a wing to make it more aerodynamic?"

Put to another use. Using an existing product or process for a new purpose. For example, you might ask "What if we used satellite technology to improve weather forecasting for air traffic control?"

Eliminate. Is removing an element of a product or process to simplify it. For example, you might ask "What if we eliminated the need for a human pilot in certain aircraft designs?"

Reverse. This is reversing the order of a process or product. You might ask "What if we started with the landing gear design and worked backwards to the rest of the aircraft design?"

For example, aerospace and aircraft design engineers can use this framework and these cues to explore new possibilities and generate ideas, you can develop innovative solutions to complex problems in aviation and aerospace.

Let me give you a few examples of how you could apply SCAMPER in aviation and aerospace:

Substitute.

How can we substitute traditional aviation fuels with more sustainable alternatives? The aviation industry is under pressure to reduce its environmental impact, and one of the most significant contributors to greenhouse gas emissions is traditional aviation fuels. By substituting them with more sustainable alternatives, we could significantly reduce the carbon footprint of aviation. For example, we could explore how to transition to hydrogen as a zero-emission fuel for aircraft. We could also investigate electric or hybrid-electric propulsion systems that use battery or fuel-cell technology, or how to improve the efficiency of alternative fuel engines through advanced materials and combustion technology.

Combine.

What if we combined the design of a helicopter with that of a fixed-wing aircraft to create a new type of vertical takeoff and landing vehicle? This could be used for a variety of applications, such as search and rescue, cargo transport, and urban air mobility.

Adapt.

How can we adapt the principles of biomimicry to improve sustainable electrical aircraft design? Biomimicry is the practice of imitating nature to solve human problems. By studying the flight patterns of birds and insects, we can learn how to improve the aerodynamics and energy efficiency of aircraft. For example, we could design aircraft wings that are inspired by the shape and structure of different types of bird wings, dolphin or fish fins or use lightweight materials that mimic the properties of butterfly or bees' wings. We could also explore how to use natural materials and processes to reduce the environmental impact of aircraft manufacturing and maintenance.

Modify.

How can we modify the design of spacecraft to improve their resilience and durability in space? Spacecraft face a range of challenges in the harsh and unpredictable environment of space, such as extreme temperatures, radiation, and micrometeoroids. By modifying their design, we could enhance their ability to withstand these challenges and improve their overall performance and longevity. For example, we could explore new materials and coatings that are more resistant to radiation and thermal stress or develop new propulsion systems that are more efficient and reliable. We could also use modular or reconfigurable designs that allow spacecraft to adapt to changing conditions or repair themselves in case of damage. By applying SCAMPER and other creative thinking techniques to spacecraft design, we can create more resilient and adaptable spacecraft that can unlock new possibilities for space exploration and discovery.

Put to other uses.

How can we put space technology and resources to other uses beyond space exploration? Space technology and resources have the potential to generate value and benefits beyond the traditional domains of space exploration and research. By putting them to other uses, we could open new opportunities for innovation and progress in various fields. For example, we could explore how to use space-based communication and navigation systems for disaster response and emergency management, or how to leverage space-based earth observation data for environmental monitoring and resource management. We could also investigate how to use space resources, such as asteroid mining, for in-situ manufacturing or space-based infrastructure development. By applying SCAMPER and other creative thinking techniques to space technology and resources, we can unlock new possibilities for the use and application of space assets that can contribute to sustainable development and human well-being on Earth.

Eliminate.

What if we eliminated the need for a human pilot in certain aircraft designs? Autonomous aircraft could be used for a variety of applications, such as cargo transport, aerial surveys, and military operations.

Reverse.

What if we started with the landing gear design and worked backwards to the rest of the aircraft design? By starting with the landing gear, we could develop more efficient and reliable aircraft that are easier to maintain and repair.

With a creative and open mindset, you can achieve excellence and make a meaningful impact on the world.

Reverse Engineering Thinking

Reverse thinking is one of my favorite creative thinking techniques. It involves looking at a problem or situation from the opposite direction, or even trying to achieve the opposite outcome. When you deliberately challenge your assumptions and flip your perspective, you can often uncover new insights and opportunities that you might have missed otherwise.

Let's say you're working on a project to develop a new aircraft engine. Instead of focusing on how to make the engine more powerful, you could start by asking: 'How can we make this engine less powerful?' This might seem counterintuitive, but it can lead to some interesting ideas. You might realize that a less powerful engine could be more efficient, or that it could be used in different types of aircraft that don't require as much power.

Another example is that you may imagine you're trying to come up with a new marketing campaign for a product that has been struggling to gain traction in the market. Instead of thinking about how to promote the product, try to approach the problem from the opposite perspective: how can you actively discourage people from buying the product?

This might sound counterintuitive, but by exploring this question, you might uncover some valuable insights. Perhaps there's a specific group of customers who would be better off not using the product, and by targeting that group with your messaging, you can improve the product's reputation among other customer segments. Or, by highlighting the product's flaws and limitations, you might actually increase its perceived value by positioning it as an honest and transparent offering.

These are just simple examples of how reverse thinking can be applied to a marketing or product design problem. The key is to approach problems from a completely different angle and see what new ideas and insights emerge. With practice, you can become adept at using this technique to break through creative blocks and generate innovative solutions.

Of course, reverse thinking is not always the best approach to every problem. Sometimes, a straightforward or analytical approach might be more appropriate. However, when you find yourself stuck or struggling to come up with new ideas, reverse thinking can be a valuable technique to add to your toolkit.

To use reverse thinking effectively you should keep an open mind and be willing to explore unconventional ideas. Don't be afraid to push the boundaries and challenge the status quo. The goal of reverse thinking is often not necessarily to come up with a solution that's the exact opposite of what you're trying to achieve, but rather to stimulate your thinking and generate new insights. Next time you're faced with a challenging problem or creative roadblock, try flipping your perspective and approaching the problem from the opposite direction. You might be surprised at the creative solutions that emerge.

Mental Rehearsal Exercise

Let's talk about a mental exercise that you can practice individually to improve your focus and performance before your work. This exercise is called the 'mental rehearsal.'

Mental rehearsal is a technique used by elite performers to prepare for a task or challenge mentally. It involves visualizing the task in your mind, going through each step in a detailed way, and imagining yourself executing each step perfectly.

To begin, find a quiet and comfortable space where you won't be interrupted. Close your eyes and take a few deep breaths to relax. It is important to reach a relaxed state whereby your mind is Visualize the task or challenge you will be facing in your work. Imagine yourself going through each step, from start to finish, and executing each step perfectly. Visualize yourself feeling confident, focused, and in control throughout the process.

You need to make the visualization as detailed as possible. Imagine the environment around you, the sensations in your body, and any sounds or smells that might be present. The more vivid and realistic the visualization, the more effective it will be.

Practice the mental rehearsal regularly before your work, and you'll find that it will help you to stay focused, calm, and confident in high-pressure situations. Mental training is just as important as physical training for achieving peak performance.

Simulation and Simulator Training

I've worked in Flight Operations and Flight Deck training for pilots at one of the world's largest airlines and we conducted many elements of the pilot training in simulators and use them to effectively prepare the crew members for their jobs.

Simulators are a crucial component of pilot training. Studies have looked at the similarities between the mental workload in each and although there are some differences, the value of training in simulators is very high.

"...measurement of mental workload in basic civil aviation training with psychophysiological methods can provide reliable data on mental work load demands during specific flight segments and for comparisons between simulator and aircraft flight. The results identify flight segments and individual maneuvers with high mental workload demands (takeoff, rejected takeoff, engine failure, Flap 7/approach, go-around, touchdown and landing) of particular importance to focus on during basic flight training. Also, overall the results confirm the training value of using simulator..."[5]

They provide a safe and controlled environment where pilots and cabin crew can practice and refine their skills and simulate emergency situations that we may encounter in real-life scenarios. Simulators can be full motion simulators, or a fixed training device and they provide the most realistic environment in which to train. They are effective because they create as close as possible the conditions and sensations that crew encounter when flying real aircraft. Space programs also use them effectively, because they prepare the astronauts for various scenarios and circumstances that they will encounter during missions. If you examine this closely, these devices do something very similar to the Mental Rehearsal exercise previously mentioned. They simulate in as much realistic detail as possible the actual work conditions and exercise items that the crew will encounter on the operations. The added benefit is cost savings and safety. The simulators, although expensive pieces of equipment, do not require fuel and if while in training something occurs that is dangerous, the crews can learn from it and avoid repeating the mistake when in the real flight operations.

Training programs are divided into several stages, starting with basic operating procedures and progressing to more complex scenarios. In the initial stages, pilots focus on developing basic skills such as takeoff and landing. As they progress, more complex scenarios are incorporated such as engine failures, system malfunctions, and other emergency situations. Simulators provide an excellent way to learn and implement standard operating procedures and to work in a team under the principles of Crew Resource Management (CRM).

"...The aviation industry has been commended for its ability to maintain a high level of safety despite operating in a mission critical, high impact work environment. This commitment to mindfulness and safely has led to the aviation community's transition to a high reliability organisation (HRO). A key factor in this transition was its commitment to team training and belief that collaboration among crew-members can be used as a key strategy by which errors can be managed. This recognition led to the development of a highly successful team training program (i.e., crew resource management, CRM)..." [6]

One key aspect of the training is the use of scenario-based training. This involves creating realistic scenarios that replicate real-world situations and challenges. This approach allows us to develop problem-solving skills and decision-making abilities, as well as building situational awareness. In addition to technical skills, a strong emphasis is placed on communication and teamwork. Work closely with your colleagues and other crew members to ensure effective communication and coordination during flight operations. Approach each session with a clear and specific set of learning objectives. This will help to focus your attention and ensure that you are making progress towards your goals.

You should be actively seeking out feedback and using simulators to refine your skills and improve your performance. Always maintain a positive attitude and a willingness to learn. Simulator training can be challenging, but with the right mindset and approach, we can develop the skills and abilities needed to excel in our jobs. As you can see there are major benefits to mental rehearsal, simulator training and practicing in realistic conditions. Your nervous system adapts to the stimuli of the environment and sets up behavioral pathways that align with the standard operating procedures you practice. Practice and training are vital in all high-level performance pursuits, and you can see this in sparring practice with boxers and mixed martial artists. When training for the Olympics the athletes even must train for the added distractions of media and crowds. They must be prepared for all that occurs when it comes to the time to execute your performance.

Design Thinking

Design thinking is a problem-solving approach that emphasizes creativity, empathy, and experimentation. It involves understanding the needs of the user, generating ideas, prototyping, and testing.

In aviation and aerospace, design thinking can be applied to a wide range of challenges, from improving aircraft design to developing new training programs. By taking a design thinking approach, we can ensure that we are creating solutions that meet the needs of the people who will be using them, and that we are constantly experimenting and iterating to improve. The key to successful design thinking is to approach problems with an open mind, stay curious, and be willing to try new things.

It's an approach that focuses on understanding the needs of the users and developing solutions that are both desirable and feasible. A human-centered approach that emphasizes empathy, experimentation, and iteration. There are several models and frameworks for implementing design thinking, but one popular model is the Stanford Design Thinking Process. It consists of five stages:

1. Empathize. This stage involves understanding the needs and perspectives of the users. It involves observing, listening, and engaging with the users to develop a deep understanding of their needs and desires.
2. Define. This stage involves synthesizing the information gathered during the empathy stage to define the problem statement. The problem statement should be specific and focused on the user's needs.
3. Ideate. This stage involves generating many ideas and potential solutions to the defined problem. The goal is to generate a wide range of ideas without judgment or criticism.
4. Prototype. This stage involves creating low-fidelity prototypes

of the most promising ideas generated during the ideation stage. The prototypes are used to test and refine the ideas.

5. Test. This stage involves testing the prototypes with the users and getting feedback. The goal is to identify what works and what needs improvement, and to refine the solution based on user feedback.

Example of Application for Emergency Training

Here is an example of a classroom interaction on how to potentially implement deign thinking in your work.

In this scenario a student Cabin Crew member discusses with me the problem of clouded thinking during a smoke in the cabin emergency.

Student: I struggle with clouded thinking during emergencies. For example, during a recent flight, we experienced smoke in the cabin and had to make an emergency landing. My mind felt scattered, and I had trouble staying calm and focused. Can design thinking help me with this?

Noel: Yes, let's start by using the design thinking process to understand the problem and identify potential solutions. How did you feel during the emergency landing?

Student: I felt panicked and overwhelmed. I couldn't think clearly, and I was worried about the safety of the passengers and crew.

Noel: Okay, so we know that the problem is a lack of clear thinking during high-pressure situations, and we have a better understanding of how that affects you and your team. The next step is to define the problem. How can we reframe the problem so that we can start to generate ideas for solutions?

Student: Well, I guess the problem is that we need a way to stay calm and focused during emergencies so that we can make the best decisions and keep everyone safe.

Noel: Great, now we're getting somewhere. The third step is to ideate or generate ideas for solutions. What are some ways that you and your team could stay calm and focused during emergencies?

Student: Maybe we could practice some breathing techniques or visualization exercises before the flight. Or we could practice more often the checklist of emergency procedures to follow so that we don't have to rely on memory alone. I could mentally rehearse several times, managing the situation well in my mind while in a relaxed state and trying to anchor that in my body and nervous system.

Noel: Those are great ideas. The fourth step is to prototype or test out those ideas. Which idea do you want to try first?

Student: I think we should start with the breathing exercises. I recall from a previous training with you the benefit of anchoring a state with a physical act like touching my thumb and forefinger together and reminding myself with autosuggestion that this will trigger my relaxation response. I've heard that can be helpful for reducing stress and anxiety.

Noel: Okay, great. The final step is to test and iterate. Try out the breathing and anchoring exercises during your next flight and see how it goes. If it works well, great. If not, we can go back to the ideation phase and come up with more ideas to try.

By using design thinking, you can approach problems in a more systematic and creative way and come up with solutions that are tailored to your specific needs and challenges. Feel free to use the Design thinking framework on a regular basis to improve your own performance.

The power of your thoughts is directly proportional to the intensity of your focus. If you can maintain unwavering focus on your goals and the actions needed to achieve them, you will unlock a level of success and achievement beyond what you ever thought possible.

Situational Awareness

Situational awareness is a term used to describe the ability of an individual to perceive and comprehend the environment around you, including the people, objects, and events that are occurring. It is a critical skill in a range of fields, including aviation, military, law enforcement, and emergency services, where accurate perception and understanding of the situation can mean the difference between success and failure. It is the ability to understand your environment including your potential threats and opportunities. Its applications can be broad, from a Captain and pilot understanding the attitude and response of their aircraft to the surrounding airspace and traffic. For cabin crew it could be the development of a potential medical emergency for a passenger unless intervention is coordinated. For an astronaut it can be the trajectory of their spacecraft and position and location relative to the flight plan.

One useful tool for enhancing situational awareness is to conduct a mental audit. This is a technique used to evaluate the current situation and identify potential problems or risks. To conduct a mental audit, individuals must be alert and mindful of their surroundings, actively seeking out information that might be relevant to their situation. They should ask themselves questions such as:

What is happening around me?

What are the potential risks or hazards?

How can I mitigate these risks?

What are my options for action?

Flight crews must maintain Situational Awareness 100% of the time. For example, if an airliner is flying in mountainous regions on approach to embedded airports below the peaks, then if the flight deck crew cannot see out the front window, they must always maintain absolute situational awareness in order to avoid dangers such as controlled flight into terrain accidents.

Here are some tips and tricks for maintaining situational awareness:

- Stay Focused. Pay attention to what's happening around you and keep your focus on the task at hand. Avoid getting distracted by your surroundings, your phone or other factors.
- Use checklists to ensure that you don't miss anything important. Checklists help you stay organized and focused, especially during critical moments.
- Be aware of any changes or deviations from the norm. Look for anomalies that might indicate a problem or a potential threat.
- Communicate Effectively. Maintain good communication with your team and other stakeholders. Share information clearly and effectively, and don't be afraid to ask questions or seek clarification.
- Anticipate Problems. Think ahead and anticipate potential problems before they occur. This allows you to plan and prepare accordingly, so you can respond quickly and effectively.
- Use Technology. Use technology to your advantage. For example, you can use electronic instruments and know exactly where you are at any given time, be aware of what VOR, DME and active waypoint you are at and constantly stay informed and up to date.
- Practice, Practice, Practice. Practice maintaining situational awareness regularly. This helps to reinforce good habits and develop muscle memory so that you can respond quickly and effectively in any situation.

Situational awareness is a skill that requires constant practice and vigilance. By using these tips and tricks, you can maintain your situational awareness and stay safe in any situation. This can also relate to layovers, for example when the crews are staying overnight at destinations away from home, know where you are going and what the safe locations and routes are at any given time. Know who you are with and even simple common-sense items like never leaving your drink unattended while you go to the restroom. That will ensure that nothing is placed in there while you are not looking, and you can remove that risk. When walking in cities you are visiting maintain situational awareness of your surrounding environment to reduce risk. Make it a habit, develop your observation skills and constantly develop the skill of identifying and eliminating threats as an instinctive process.

Strategic Review

The military concept of a strategic review is another useful tool for enhancing situational awareness. This involves taking a step back from the immediate situation and evaluating the broader context in which it is occurring. A strategic review might include a SWOT analysis, which is a framework for evaluating strengths, weaknesses, opportunities, and threats. This analysis can help individuals to identify their own strengths and weaknesses, as well as external factors that might affect their situation.

Understanding where you are right now is an essential part of designing a strategic plan going forward. This requires an honest assessment of your current situation, including your strengths and weaknesses, your resources, and your limitations. Once you have a clear understanding of your current situation, you can begin to formulate a plan for moving forward. This plan should consider your goals and objectives, as well as the external factors that might impact on your success.

The process is designed to help you understand where you are right now, and in order to design a strategic plan going forward.

Let me give you an overview of the framework. First, you need to identify your mission and objectives. This means defining what you want to achieve and why it's important to you. You also need to have a clear understanding of your personal values and beliefs.

Next, conduct a SWOT analysis. This is an evaluation of your strengths, weaknesses, opportunities, and threats. It's important to be truthful with yourself in this step and identify areas where you need improvement.

Then, conduct a situational analysis. This involves reviewing your current circumstances and understanding the factors that are affecting your progress towards your goals. This includes analyzing your environment, your resources, and your competitors.

Then develop a strategic plan. Based on your mission, objectives, SWOT analysis, and situational analysis, you should develop a plan that outlines specific actions that you will take to achieve your goals. For instance, if you're a pilot, you might assess your strengths in flying skills, your weaknesses in communication, opportunities for training and career advancement, and threats such as weather and technical issues and your knowledge of how to address them. A strategic review framework can help you achieve success in any field, including the aviation and space industry. It provides a structured way to assess your current situation, identify opportunities for improvement, and develop a plan to achieve your goals.

Decision Models and Decision Making

I would like to introduce the process of decision making that Benjamin Franklin designed and found to be effective in his own life. This process has been tested time and time again, and I believe it will be of great value to you as well. The method may be called the "Pro and Con" method. Benjamin Franklin's decision-making process involves breaking down a decision into a list of pros and cons. He believed that by listing out the potential positive and negative outcomes of a decision, it would be easier to evaluate which option was the best. Once you have the list of all the pros and cons of a decision.

To use this method, start by listing out all the potential positive outcomes (pros) of the decision. Then, list out all the potential negative outcomes (cons) of the decision. Once you have a comprehensive list of pros and cons, evaluate each item on the list to determine its significance and likelihood of occurring and then assign a weight to each item based on its importance to you and your goal.

After evaluating each item on the list, you can tally up the number of pros and cons and compare them to determine which option has more weight. Franklin believed that this process would help to clarify a decision and make it easier to identify the best course of action.

The following is an example of how it can be applied to deciding which route to take for the Apollo 11 mission to the moon:

Step	Description	Example for Apollo 11
1	Define the decision to be made	The decision is to determine which route to take to reach the moon
2	Gather information and identify alternatives	Consider all possible routes and gather data on factors such as fuel consumption, travel time, and safety for each route
3	Identify pros and cons of each alternative	Pros: Shorter travel time, less fuel consumption. Cons: Higher risk of encountering space debris, more dangerous landing.
4	Weight the pros and cons	Based on the information gathered, weigh the pros and cons of each alternative.
5	Decide	After weighing the pros and cons, decide which route to take based on which one has the most favorable outcome.
6	Implement the decision	Put the chosen route into action and make any necessary adjustments along the way.
7	Evaluate the decision	After the mission, evaluate the decision made and consider if there were any other factors that could have been considered for future reference.

Table 1.0

Example Apollo 11

Step	Description	Example for Apollo 11
1	Define the decision to be made	The decision is to determine which route to take to reach the moon
2	Gather information and identify alternatives	Consider all possible routes and gather data on factors such as fuel consumption, travel time, and safety for each route. Alternatives: Direct approach, circumlunar, and Earth orbit rendezvous.
3	Identify pros and cons of each alternative	Direct approach: Pros - Shorter travel time, less fuel consumption (weighting 6.5). Cons - Higher risk of encountering space debris, more dangerous landing (weighting 9). Circumlunar: Pros - Lower risk of encountering space debris, safer landing (weighting 6.4). Cons - Longer travel time, more fuel consumption (weighting 8). Earth orbit rendezvous: Pros - Safe landing, lower fuel consumption (weighting 9.2) Cons - Longer travel time, more complex maneuvering (weighting 5.7).
4	Weight the pros and cons	Based on the information gathered, weigh the pros and cons of each alternative. Direct approach: Pros outweigh the cons, but higher risk. Circumlunar: Safe but longer travel time and more fuel consumption. Earth orbit rendezvous: Safe and lower fuel consumption, but more complex maneuvering.
5	Decide	After weighing the pros and cons, decide to take the Earth orbit rendezvous route.
6	Implement the decision	Put the chosen route into action and make any necessary adjustments along the way.
7	Evaluate the decision	After the mission, evaluate the decision made and consider if there were any other factors that could be considered for future reference. Evaluation is favorable in this case as borne out in the successful mission.

Table 2.0

Modern cutting-edge decision-making models are rooted in the fields of psychology, neuroscience, and artificial intelligence. These models emphasize the importance of data-driven, evidence-based decision-making, and utilize advanced technologies to analyze complex datasets and identify patterns and trends that would be difficult for humans to detect on their own.

One such model is the use of machine learning algorithms to identify patterns and make predictions based on large datasets. These algorithms can be trained to recognize patterns in a variety of contexts, from financial markets to medical diagnosis.

Another modern model is based on the concept of "decision intelligence," which involves a systematic approach to decision-making that incorporates multiple factors, including human intuition, data analysis, and collaborative decision-making. Decision intelligence aims to balance the strengths of human and machine intelligence, combining human creativity and problem-solving skills with the speed and accuracy of machine learning algorithms.

Other modern decision-making models include the use of big data analytics, which involves the collection and analysis of vast amounts of data from a variety of sources, and the use of predictive modeling, which involves the use of statistical algorithms to identify patterns and make predictions about future outcomes.

In aviation and aerospace, the most effective decision-making models are those that prioritize safety and efficiency. One such model is Crew Resource Management (CRM), which was first introduced in the 1970s by the National Aeronautics and Space Administration (NASA). CRM emphasizes the importance of communication, situational awareness, and teamwork in decision-making, particularly in high-stress environments.

A model used in aviation and aerospace is the Threat and Error Management (TEM) model, which focuses on identifying and mitigating threats and errors before they lead to accidents or incidents. The TEM model emphasizes the importance of identifying potential threats and errors, analyzing their potential impact, and taking proactive measures to address them.

The elements of Threat and Error Management (TEM)

Element of TEM	Description
Threats	Factors or conditions that have the potential to impact the safety of a flight, such as weather, equipment malfunctions, or communication breakdowns
Errors	Human actions or decisions that result in deviations from intended actions, such as miscommunications, incorrect procedures, or violations of regulations
Mitigations	Actions taken to reduce the likelihood or impact of threats or errors, such as implementing checklists, cross-checking procedures, or utilizing backup systems
Situational Awareness	Understanding of the current state of the flight, including factors such as altitude, speed, location, weather conditions, and the status of equipment
Decision Making	The process of identifying available options, evaluating their potential outcomes, and selecting the best course of action based on the situation
Communication	The exchange of information between crew members, air traffic control, and other relevant parties, including clear and concise transmission of critical information
Leadership	The ability of the captain or other designated leader to effectively manage and direct the crew in response to changing conditions or challenges, including the ability to recognize and address potential errors or threats

Table 3.0

Aeronautical Decision Making

ADM stands for Aeronautical Decision Making, and it is a framework used by pilots to make effective and safe decisions in the aviation environment. The FAA (Federal Aviation Administration) defines ADM as a systematic approach to the mental process used by aircraft pilots to consistently determine the best course of action in response to a given set of circumstances.

ADM is based on the principles of decision making and risk management, and it is designed to help pilots make effective decisions by considering all available information and factors, assessing the potential consequences of different courses of action, and selecting the course of action that is most appropriate for the situation.

The ADM framework consists of various steps that help the crew members in:

1. Identifying personal attitudes hazardous to safe flight
2. Learning behavior modification techniques
3. Learning and applying the principles of risk management
4. Evaluating the effectiveness of one's ADM skills.
5. Identifying and mitigating stress
6. Developing and maintaining situational awareness

ADM is taught as part of pilot training, and it is considered a critical component of safe flight operations. By using ADM, pilots can identify and manage risks, make effective decisions, and ensure safe flight operations. Effective decision-making models in aviation and aerospace are those that prioritize safety, emphasize teamwork and communication, and provide a structured approach to decision-making.

The Federal Aviation Administration (FAA) has introduced the 3-P Model, a three-step systematic approach to help pilots effectively apply the principles of Aeronautical Decision Making (ADM) during all phases of flight. The 3-P Model, comprising of *Perceive, Process, and Perform*, provides a structured framework for accomplishing each ADM task.

Perceive

In order to apply this model, pilots must first perceive the given set of circumstances for their flight. This includes gathering all relevant information pertaining to the flight, which allows them to comprehend the mission and environment in which it will be conducted. This crucial step starts during preflight preparations and continues throughout the flight.

Process

Once the information is perceived, pilots must process it by analyzing its impact on flight safety and determining the best course of action. This process is not a one-time event, but an ongoing analysis as new information becomes available during the flight.

Perform

Pilots must perform the implementation of the best course of action. The results of the performance become new information that is perceived and analyzed, and based on those results, pilots will decide whether to continue with the action or make a change. The 3-P Model provides a structured, methodical approach to aid pilots in making effective decisions and maintaining safety during flight.

The ADM process on involves identifying several crucial factors, including the ability to:

- Recognize changes or lack of changes in circumstances.
- Identify any personal biases that may affect decision making.
- Maintain honesty about one's own abilities and limitations.
- Establish and stick to personal minimums for safety.
- Resist external pressures, such as the temptation to save time, money, or avoid embarrassment.
- Create and implement a contingency plan in case of unexpected events.
- Continuously evaluate the outcomes of decisions made.

OODA Loop decision mental model used in combat flying.

Imagine you're a pilot flying in less-than-ideal weather conditions, and you're trying to determine whether it's safe to continue the flight or if you should divert to another airport. One principle from aviation psychology that can help guide your decision-making is the "OODA loop." OODA stands for Observe, Orient, Decide, Act, and it's a framework for making quick and effective decisions in high-pressure situations.

Here's how you could apply the OODA loop in this scenario:

Observe

Take a close look at the current weather conditions, including visibility, wind speed and direction, precipitation, and cloud cover. Consider how these conditions may affect your ability to safely operate the aircraft.

Orient

Based on your observations, assess the current situation and understand the potential risks and benefits of continuing the flight versus diverting. Consider factors such as the distance to the nearest airport, the capabilities of the aircraft, and the experience level of the crew.

Decide

Based on your assessment, make a clear and informed decision about whether to continue the flight or divert to another airport. Be sure to communicate your decision with the rest of the crew and any relevant air traffic control personnel.

Act

Execute your decision, whether that means continuing the flight or initiating a diversion. Make any necessary adjustments to the flight plan and continue to monitor weather conditions and other factors that may affect the safety of the flight.

By applying the OODA loop in this situation, you can make a more informed and effective decision, with a greater chance of achieving a safe outcome.

Mental Approaches to Top Performance

The compound effect is the principle that small actions, consistently taken over time, can lead to significant results. This principle is based on the idea that success is not the result of a single action or event, but rather the accumulation of many small actions that are taken consistently over a period of time. By consistently taking small actions, we can create a positive momentum that leads to greater results than any one action on its own. Like diverging lines with a slight angle of difference, the effect may not appear significant in the beginning however as one extends out further in time the effect becomes greater. The key to benefiting from the compound effect is consistency. For example, a couple of degrees divergence of a flight path of an airliner departing Washington heading west will significantly alter the arrival point when it reaches the west coast unless corrected along the way. When we consistently take small actions towards a goal, we build momentum that makes it easier to continue taking those actions. Over time, the impact of those actions becomes greater, and we begin to see significant results.

For example, let's say a group of athletes wants to improve their performance in their sport. Instead of trying to make drastic changes to their training or technique, they focus on making small improvements in their daily habits. They might focus on getting an extra 30 minutes of sleep each night, eating a healthier diet, and practicing a specific skill for just a few minutes each day. While each of these actions on their own might not seem significant, over time, they can lead to a significant improvement in performance. The compound effect can also work in reverse. If we consistently make small negative choices, over time, the impact of those choices can become significant. For example, if we consistently eat unhealthy food and don't exercise, over time, we may begin to experience negative health consequences. The concept of aggregating actions and making constant marginal adjustments is a powerful tool for improving performance in any field. It is a simple but effective approach that involves breaking down complex tasks into smaller, more manageable steps and then making small, incremental changes to improve performance over time.

One of the keys to successfully using this approach is to have a clear understanding of the goals and objectives that you are trying to achieve. This requires a deep understanding of your discipline and the specific skills and knowledge that are required to be successful in it. Once you have a clear understanding of your goals, you can begin to break down the complex tasks into smaller, more manageable steps. This allows you to focus on one task at a time and make incremental improvements as you go. Another aspect of this approach is the need to constantly monitor and evaluate your performance. This requires a high degree of self-awareness and the ability to objectively assess your strengths and weaknesses. In this way, you can identify areas where you need to make improvements and then make the necessary adjustments to your approach.

Over time, these small, incremental improvements can add up to significant gains in performance. By constantly aggregating your actions and making marginal adjustments, you can reach top performance in your discipline. By creating the right habits that favor the outcomes you want, time will be your friend and each passing day takes you closer to your aims.

Developing good habits and routines is essential for achieving excellence. This means setting aside time each day to work towards your goals, and creating a consistent routine that helps you stay on track. I recommend starting your day with a positive mindset and taking time each day to reflect on your progress and accomplishments.

Another important factor in pursuing excellence is surrounding yourself with positive influences. Collaboration and feedback from others can help you refine your skills and improve your performance over time. Excellence is not a destination, but a journey. It requires continuous effort and improvement over time. Embrace the process of learning and growth, and don't be afraid to take risks and try new things. With dedication and perseverance, you can achieve excellence in your professional and personal life.

Set up an encouraging environment to instill a growth mindset:

- *Surround yourself with positive cues.* Fill your workspace or home with motivational quotes, pictures of people who inspire you, or reminders of your goals. Seeing these positive cues can help reinforce a growth mindset and keep you motivated. Put a reminder of your goal in your mirror so you will see it in the morning as you brush your teeth, and again in the evening.
- *Find a role model.* Identify someone who embodies the qualities and traits you admire and strive to emulate them. Having a role model can provide a sense of direction and inspiration. You may even strive to surpass their achievements.
- *Celebrate progress.* Acknowledge and celebrate your progress, even if it's small. This can help keep you motivated and reinforce the idea that growth is possible.
- *Embrace challenges.* View challenges as opportunities for growth rather than obstacles to overcome. This can help shift your mindset from a fixed to a growth perspective.
- *Focus on learning.* Emphasize the process of learning rather than the result. This can help you stay motivated and enjoy the journey towards achieving your goals.
- *Surround yourself with positive people.* Surround yourself with people who support and encourage your growth. Having a supportive network can provide a sense of community and accountability.

You can also create positive habits by setting up a routine or schedule that works for you. This can include things like setting aside time for exercise or meditation or establishing a consistent sleep schedule. By making these activities a regular part of your day, you'll be more likely to stick to them and reap the benefits.

Surround yourself with supportive people. Whether it's colleagues, friends, or family members, having a supportive network can make all the difference in your pursuit of excellence. Seek out people who share your values and goals, and who will encourage and motivate you along the way.

Mind Tricks of the Samurai

The samurai were known for their discipline, focus, and calmness under pressure. One technique they used to achieve this state was called "mushin," which translates to "no mind" or "empty mind." This concept refers to a state of mind where one is completely present in the moment and free from distraction, anxiety, or fear.

To achieve mushin, the samurai would engage in various forms of meditation, visualization, and physical training. They would practice breathing exercises to calm their minds and visualize themselves succeeding in their tasks. They would also engage in physical training to condition their bodies and minds to remain calm under stress.

Samurai practiced "*zanshin*," which means "remaining mind" or "lingering mind." This concept refers to the state of mind where one remains alert and focused even after the task at hand is complete. The samurai believed that maintaining this state of mind was crucial to being prepared for any unexpected events. They would remain aware of their surroundings and potential threats, even in seemingly peaceful situations. They would also practice remaining calm and focused even after completing a task, as a way of maintaining their readiness for any new challenges that may arise. When out of base practice *zanshin*! We will look at this again a little later in the book.

Wu Wei Approach for Cabin Crew

Wu Wei is a concept in Taoism that refers to effortless action or non-action. It is a state of being in which one can act spontaneously and effectively, without overthinking or forcing things to happen. In the context of aviation and aerospace, *wu wei* can be applied in situations where quick decisions and actions are required.

As a cabin crew member, you can use *wu wei* to focus and perform at your best. For example, when dealing with a challenging passenger or unexpected situation, instead of reacting impulsively or aggressively, you can pause and take a deep breath to center yourself. Allow your actions to flow naturally and without force, using your training and experience to guide you. By staying calm and in control, you can handle the situation with ease and grace, and maintain a positive and professional demeanor.

W*u wei* is not about being passive or indifferent, but rather about responding to situations in a way that is efficient, effective, and aligned with your values and goals as a cabin crew member. Regular practice of *wu wei* can improve your performance and enhance your ability to provide excellent service to your passengers.

Wu wei is the art of effortless action, and it can be practiced in many ways. As cabin crew, one way to practice *wu wei* is to focus on your breath and body awareness during your daily routine.

For example, when serving passengers, instead of rushing through the motions and feeling stressed, try to remain calm and focused on your breath. Pay attention to the way your body moves and feels as you walk down the aisle, serve drinks, or pick up items. By remaining present in the moment and letting go of any distractions or worries, you can perform your duties with ease and flow.

Another way to practice *wu wei* as cabin crew is to cultivate a sense of detachment from any negative emotions or stressful situations that may arise during your work. Instead of getting caught up in the drama or feeling overwhelmed, try to remain calm and centered. Focus on your breath, visualize a positive outcome, and trust in your training and experience to guide you through any challenges.

Wu wei is not about doing nothing, but about finding a state of flow and effortless action. By practicing these methods, you can perform at your best and provide the highest level of service to your passengers.

Exercise

One exercise that the cabin crew can practice cultivating *wu wei* is mindful breathing. This involves sitting in a quiet space perhaps when you are on a short break in your Jumspeat and focusing on your breath, allowing thoughts to come and go without judgment or attachment.

To begin, find a quiet place to sit comfortably with your back straight and feet flat on the ground. Close your eyes or lower your gaze and bring your attention to your breath. Notice the sensation of the air moving in and out of your nostrils or the rise and fall of your chest and abdomen.

Allow your breath to flow naturally, without trying to control it. As thoughts arise, simply acknowledge them and let them go, returning your attention to your breath. If you find your mind wandering, gently bring your attention back to your breath, without judging yourself.

Practice this exercise for a few minutes each day, gradually increasing the duration over time. By regularly practicing mindful breathing, you can cultivate a state of calm and clarity that can help you navigate challenging situations with greater ease and effectiveness.

Yoga for Wellbeing

Yoga can be a valuable tool for managing stress, improving mental health, and promoting overall wellbeing and a powerful tool for promoting mental clarity and focus. Explore the many different forms of yoga and to find a practice that works for you. Whether it is a gentle restorative practice, a dynamic vinyasa flow, or a more meditative style, there is a form of yoga that can benefit everyone. Yoga, the ancient practice of union with the divine, offers a holistic approach to mental training that can help you manage stress, increase your mental clarity, and enhance your overall well-being. The practice of yoga encompasses various techniques, including physical postures (asanas), breathing exercises (pranayama), meditation (dhyana), and ethical guidelines (yamas and niyamas). The practice of pranayama, or controlled breathing, is particularly effective in reducing stress and calming the mind. By bringing your attention to your breath, you can slow down your heart rate, lower your blood pressure, and enter a state of deep relaxation. Practicing pranayama before a flight or during a break can help you manage anxiety, increase focus, and improve your performance.

The practice of meditation, or dhyana, deals with training your mind to stay focused on a single point of attention, such as your breath, a mantra, or an object. Regular meditation practice can help you reduce mental distractions, enhance your concentration, and cultivate a sense of inner peace and calm.

Yoga is not just a physical practice; it is a holistic approach to mental, physical, and spiritual well-being. The practice of yoga can help you cultivate a deeper connection with yourself, with others, and with the divine. It can help you develop a sense of inner peace, joy, and fulfillment that can transform your life, both on and off the job.

As aviation and aerospace professionals, you have a unique opportunity to serve humanity and contribute to the greater good.

Embracing the practice of yoga permits you to enhance your mental and physical abilities and cultivate a deeper sense of purpose and fulfillment in your work and in your life.

Exercise

One of the fundamental principles of yoga is the practice of being fully present and engaged in the moment. This can be a powerful tool for improving mental health.

- To begin, I invite you all to find a comfortable seated position with your feet flat on the ground and your hands resting on your knees. Close your eyes and take a few deep breaths, feeling your belly expand as you inhale and contract as you exhale.
- Now, begin to scan your body, starting at the top of your head and working your way down to your toes. Notice any areas of tension or discomfort and see if you can consciously release them as you exhale.
- As you continue to breathe deeply and scan your body, notice any thoughts or emotions that arise. Instead of getting caught up in them or trying to push them away, simply observe them without judgment, and then let them go as you exhale.
- Bring your awareness to your breath. Notice the sensation of the air moving in and out of your nostrils, the rise and fall of your chest and belly, and the sound of your breath.
- As you continue to breathe deeply and mindfully, imagine a sense of peace and calm washing over you, like a warm, gentle wave. Allow yourself to fully immerse in this feeling of peace and relaxation for a few moments.
- When you are ready, gently open your eyes and take a few more deep breaths before returning to your day.

Concept of Transcendental Meditation Practice

Here is a form of meditation that involves sitting comfortably with your eyes closed and silently repeating a mantra, a sound or word, for about 20 minutes. The mantra is chosen based on a specific formula, and it is meant to be used as a tool to help you transcend, or go beyond, your thoughts and reach a state of deep relaxation and inner calm.

- To begin, find a comfortable seated position with your back straight and your feet flat on the ground. Close your eyes and take a few deep breaths, feeling your belly expand as you inhale and contract as you exhale.
- Start repeating your chosen mantra silently to yourself. It is important to keep the mantra to yourself, and not to vocalize it out loud or focus too much on its meaning. Simply let it be a gentle anchor for your mind.
- As you continue to repeat the mantra, thoughts and distractions may arise, this is completely normal. Instead of trying to push them away or engage with them, simply acknowledge them and return your focus to the mantra.
- Allow yourself to fully immerse in the repetition of the mantra, letting go of any tension or stress in your body and mind.
- After about 20 minutes, gently stop repeating the mantra and take a few deep breaths, feeling the sense of calm and inner peace that comes from the practice.
- The practice of TM is something that can be done twice a day, for 20 minutes each time. It is a simple yet powerful tool that can help you manage stress, improve mental health and wellbeing, and achieve greater clarity and focus in all aspects of your life.

Equanimity

Equanimity is a mental state of calmness and composure, even during challenging situations. To achieve equanimity, try this practical exercise.

- Begin by acknowledging and accepting the current situation, whatever it may be.
- Take a few deep breaths to calm your mind and body.
- Imagine yourself as an observer, watching the situation from a distance without getting emotionally caught up in it.
- Practice non-judgmental awareness of your thoughts and emotions, simply observing them without attaching to them or trying to change them.
- Cultivate a sense of inner peace and balance, reminding yourself that you have the strength and resilience to handle whatever comes your way.

With practice, this exercise can help you develop a greater sense of equanimity, allowing you to stay centered and focused even in the midst of challenging circumstances.

Compartmentalization Strategy

Compartmentalization is a mental strategy that can help flight crews effectively deal with the stresses and demands of their job. It involves mentally separating different aspects of one's life or work into distinct compartments, so that issues in one compartment do not spill over into another. For example, a flight crew member may encounter a difficult passenger on a flight, but they can mentally "compartmentalize" that experience and leave it behind when they exit the aircraft, not allowing it to impact their personal life or future work.

To use compartmentalization effectively, flight crews can follow these steps:

- Identify the compartments. Start by identifying the different aspects of your life or work that may need to be compartmentalized. For flight crews, this may include work-related stressors, personal life stressors, and other issues that may arise during travel.
- Set boundaries. Once you have identified the different compartments, set boundaries between them. This can involve creating physical and mental barriers to help prevent issues from one compartment from affecting another.
- Practice meditation. Be mindful of your thoughts and emotions as you move between compartments. Take time to acknowledge and process any negative emotions before leaving one compartment and entering another.
- Stay focused. When you are in one compartment, stay focused on that compartment and avoid letting issues from other compartments distract you. This can help you be more present and effective in each compartment.

By practicing compartmentalization, flight crews can better manage stress and stay focused on their job, while also maintaining a healthy work-life balance.

Qigong for Aviation and Aerospace Professionals

Qigong is a physical and mental practice that originated in China and involves gentle movements, controlled breathing, and meditation. It is believed to improve the flow of vital energy (qi) throughout the body, leading to improved physical health and mental well-being. As a flight crew member, practicing qigong can help you manage stress, improve your focus and concentration, and boost your overall energy levels.

Here is a simple Qigong Exercise that you can try:

Find a quiet and comfortable place where you can stand or sit with your feet shoulder-width apart and your spine straight.

- Take a few deep breaths and focus your attention on your breath. Slowly inhale through your nose and exhale through your mouth.
- Begin to gently sway your body from side to side, letting your arms hang loosely by your sides.
- As you sway, imagine that your body is a tree, and your arms are branches swaying in the wind. Feel the gentle movement of your body and let yourself relax into it.
- As you continue to sway, imagine that you are releasing any tension or stress that you may be holding in your body. Let go of any thoughts or worries and simply focus on the sensation of movement.
- After a few minutes, slowly come to a stop and take a few deep breaths. Notice how you feel in your body and mind.

This exercise can be done for just a few minutes at a time and can be a valuable tool for managing stress and improving your overall well-being. Although you wont do this in front of other crew or passengers, you can take opportunities at your hotel room or suitable locations and moments.

Relaxation Response

The relaxation response is an effect elicited by a method developed in a study by Herbert Benson, John F. Beary & Mark P. Carol (1974)[7] based on meditation practices, it can help bring about some beneficial effects such as lower blood pressure and can help reduce stress and promote relaxation. To elicit this response, here are some steps you can take:

- Find a quiet and comfortable place to sit or lie down.
- Close your eyes and take a deep breath in, filling your lungs with air.
- Slowly exhale and let go of any tension you may be holding.
- Focus on a calming word, phrase or image. This could be anything that helps you feel relaxed and at ease.
- As you breathe in, say the word or phrase silently to yourself, and as you breathe out, let go of any tension in your body.
- Continue to focus on your word, phrase or image and allow your mind to relax and become still.
- If your mind wanders, gently bring your attention back to your word, phrase or image.

Practice this technique for at least 10-20 minutes each day.

This technique can be especially useful to recalibrate after stressful situations, such as heavy turbulence or dealing with difficult passengers. By regularly practicing the relaxation response, you can learn to access a state of relaxation and calm more easily, which can help you remain focused and alert during flights.

The relaxation response has been shown to have numerous health benefits. It can help reduce stress and anxiety, lower blood pressure, decrease heart rate, improve digestion and sleep, and reduce symptoms of conditions such as depression, chronic pain, and headaches. It can also help boost the immune system and increase overall feelings of well-being. By eliciting the relaxation response on a regular basis, flight crews can improve their physical and mental health, leading to better performance and a more fulfilling lifestyle.

Importance of Joy and a Sense of Humor

Maintaining joy and humor is crucial for the flight crews, especially during long flights or in stressful situations. Joy and humor have been shown to have several positive effects on both physical and mental health. Laughter and joy can reduce stress levels by releasing endorphins, which are natural painkillers and mood elevators. This, in turn, can reduce the risk of stress-related illnesses and improve overall well-being. Maintaining a positive attitude and sense of humor can improve social connections and relationships with others, which is especially important for a crew that must work closely together in a high-pressure environment. Humor and joy can enhance creativity and problem-solving abilities, allowing crew members to approach challenges with a more positive and innovative mindset. To keep a sense of joy and humor, the flight crews can try simple practices such as sharing jokes or funny stories, taking breaks to engage in enjoyable activities, and practicing gratitude by focusing on positive experiences and aspects of their work. It's important to remember that joy and humor are not only beneficial for the individuals, but also for the overall atmosphere and morale of the crew. By prioritizing these aspects, the flight crews can create a positive and supportive working environment, which can ultimately enhance their performance.

Laughter has been shown to decrease stress hormones and increase immune cells and infection-fighting antibodies. It also triggers the release of endorphins, the body's natural feel-good chemicals, which can promote an overall sense of well-being. Humor can serve as a coping mechanism in difficult situations, helping to reduce anxiety and tension. It can also improve social connections, as humor is often used to bond with others and create a positive, lighthearted atmosphere.

A positive, joyful attitude can lead to increased motivation and productivity, as it can help individuals approach tasks with a sense of enthusiasm and optimism. It's just better all round if you enjoy your work and being in the company of your colleagues.

Using humor can be an effective way to diffuse tension and reduce stress in many situations, including highly stressful environments. Humor can help to break down barriers, build rapport, and create a more relaxed atmosphere. For example, in the context of emergency medicine, humor can also help to ease patients' fears and anxieties and help them to feel more comfortable and confident in the care they are receiving. One of the key benefits of humor is that it can help to shift our perspective and reframe our thinking. When we are stressed or anxious, we tend to become narrowly focused on the problem at hand, which can make it difficult to see other possibilities or solutions. Humor can help to broaden our perspective and create a more flexible and creative mindset. Pay a little homage to levity, give it some quarter.

Humor is that it can help to build resilience and coping skills. By learning to laugh at ourselves and find humor in difficult situations, we can become more resilient and better able to cope with stress and adversity. In emergency medicine, where healthcare professionals are often exposed to traumatic or emotionally challenging situations, developing resilience and coping skills is critical for maintaining well-being and avoiding burnout. Similarly in aviation, and especially military aviation in the air force and naval service the same applications can be made.

However, it's important to use humor appropriately and sensitively in the context of the situation and environment. Humor should never be used at the expense of customers or colleagues, and professionals should be mindful of cultural and individual differences in humor preferences. When used effectively, humor can be a powerful tool for diffusing tension, reducing stress, and improving patient and even passenger outcomes in enhancing their experience.

Here's an example of how humor has helped Health care professionals and can do the same for you.

- Icebreaker. Humor can be used as an icebreaker to build rapport with patients and put them at ease. A well-timed joke or humorous comment can help to break down barriers and create a more relaxed atmosphere.
- Distraction. Humor can be used as a distraction technique to help patients manage pain, anxiety, or other symptoms. By diverting the patient's attention away from their symptoms, healthcare professionals can help to reduce their distress and improve their overall experience.
- Team building. Humor can be used to build camaraderie and teamwork among healthcare professionals. By finding humor in the challenges and stresses of emergency medicine, healthcare professionals can create a sense of shared experience and develop stronger relationships with their colleagues.
- Coping mechanism. Humor can be a powerful coping mechanism for healthcare professionals who are exposed to traumatic or emotionally challenging situations. By finding humor in difficult situations, healthcare professionals can reduce their stress and improve their well-being.

It's easy to draw the parallels between the professions and what works in one profession can be applied in another, whether it's used by the police, fire service, emergency departments or flight crews.

SECTION 2
WELLBEING FOR PERSONAL EXCELLENCE

The Three Pillars of Wellbeing

A. Body: Biological Aspect of Wellbeing

Our physical health is a critical component of our overall wellbeing. The body pillar of wellbeing involves taking care of our physical needs, including exercise, healthy eating, getting enough sleep, and avoiding harmful substances. By maintaining a healthy body, we can reduce the risk of developing physical illnesses, improve our energy levels and mental clarity, and enhance our ability to cope with stress.

B. Mind: Psychological Aspect of Wellbeing

Our psychological wellbeing is just as important as our physical health. The mind pillar of wellbeing involves taking care of our mental health, including managing stress, cultivating positive emotions, developing healthy coping mechanisms, and addressing any mental health conditions. By prioritizing our mental wellbeing, we can improve our ability to manage challenges, enhance our relationships, and increase our overall life satisfaction.

C. Social: Social Aspect of Wellbeing

The social pillar of wellbeing involves our social connections and relationships. Our social networks are a critical aspect of our overall wellbeing, and studies have shown that individuals with strong social support systems tend to have better physical and mental health outcomes. By prioritizing our social connections, we can reduce feelings of loneliness and isolation, increase our sense of belonging and purpose, and improve our overall wellbeing.

Interdependence of the Three Pillars

The three pillars of wellbeing are interdependent. Neglecting one pillar can have a negative impact on the other two, and improving one pillar can positively impact the others. For example, engaging in regular exercise not only benefits our physical health but can also enhance our mood and reduce stress levels, positively impacting our mental and social wellbeing. Similarly, cultivating positive social connections can provide a sense of purpose and belonging, which can enhance our physical and mental wellbeing. In order to achieve optimal wellbeing, it is essential to prioritize all three pillars and take a holistic approach to health and wellness. This can involve developing healthy habits and routines that support each pillar, seeking support from healthcare professionals or mental health professionals when necessary, and building and maintaining positive social connections. By prioritizing our overall wellbeing, we can enhance our ability to cope with life's challenges, increase our resilience, and experience greater joy and fulfillment in our daily lives.

How the Three Pillars of Wellbeing can be Applied to Flight Crews.

A. Body. The biological aspect of wellbeing is crucial for flight crews as they need to maintain good physical health in order to perform their duties effectively. This includes getting adequate sleep, staying hydrated, and eating nutritious foods. They can make sure to prioritize rest during layovers, bring healthy snacks on flights, and stretch or do light exercise during breaks to keep their bodies feeling good.

B. Mind. The psychological aspect of wellbeing is also important for flight crews as they need to be able to handle stress and maintain focus during long flights. They can practice mindfulness or meditation techniques to help calm their minds, utilize stress-management tools like deep breathing exercises, and make sure to take breaks to rest and recharge as needed.

C. Social. The social aspect of wellbeing involves maintaining positive relationships and a sense of connection with others. Flight crews can foster a sense of community within their team by supporting and encouraging each other, as well as trying to connect with passengers in a positive and friendly way.

D. Interdependence. It's important to note that these three pillars are interconnected and influence each other. For example, if a flight crew member is feeling physically unwell, this can also affect their mental and emotional wellbeing. Similarly, if there is tension or conflict within the team, this can also impact their overall wellbeing and performance. Therefore, it's important for flight crews to prioritize all three pillars in order to achieve optimal wellbeing and performance.

Recent research by (Santilhano, W., Bor, R., Hewitt M. 2019) underscores the importance of developing a more integrated definition of safety in aviation that incorporates supporting the mental health and well-being of pilots.[8]

Recommendations of how the Lessons on Improving Wellbeing can be Applied to the Flight Crews:

A. Self-awareness:

- Take time to reflect on your own wellbeing regularly, using tools such as self-assessment questionnaires or journaling.
- Identify your own strengths and weaknesses related to wellbeing and set specific goals for improvement.
- Seek feedback from colleagues or supervisors to gain additional insight and *perspective.*

B. Identifying triggers and sources of stress:

- Keep a stress diary to track when and where stress occurs, as well as the associated symptoms.
- Identify common triggers of stress, such as long flights or difficult passengers, and develop strategies to minimize their impact.
- Seek support from colleagues or supervisors when dealing with particularly challenging situations.

C. Lifestyle factors that impact wellbeing:

Focus on getting enough sleep, exercise, and a balanced diet to maintain physical wellbeing.

Seek out opportunities for social connection and community involvement to promote social wellbeing.

Prioritize time for hobbies, relaxation, and self-care activities to promote psychological wellbeing.

D. Coping strategies for stress and anxiety:

Practice relaxation techniques such as deep breathing or meditation.

Use cognitive-behavioral strategies to challenge negative thoughts and reframe situations in a more positive light. Cognitive-behavioral therapy (CBT) is a type of psychotherapy that can be helpful for the flight crews to manage their mental health and cope with the unique stressors associated with their profession. CBT is based on the idea that our thoughts, feelings, and behaviors are interconnected, and that by changing one of these components, we can change the others.

In the context of flight crews, CBT can be useful in addressing specific issues related to their job, such as anxiety related to training or flying with difficult colleagues or dealing with difficult passengers. CBT can also be used to address more general issues such as managing anxiety and improving self-esteem.

One technique used in CBT is cognitive restructuring, which involves identifying negative thoughts and replacing them with more positive and realistic ones. For example, if a flight crew member has a negative thought about their ability to handle an emergency, a CBT therapist might help them reframe that thought by asking for evidence that supports their negative thought and then challenging that evidence with more realistic thoughts.

Another method used in CBT is behavioral activation, which involves engaging in positive activities that can improve mood and reduce stress. For example, a flight crew member might be encouraged to engage in regular exercise or hobbies that they enjoy promoting physical and mental wellbeing.

Cognitive-behavioral therapy (CBT) can also be helpful for pilots who are experiencing stress related to the potential of failing a line check or exam and losing their license and livelihood. CBT is a form of therapy that focuses on changing negative thought patterns and behaviors that may be contributing to stress, anxiety, or other mental health issues.

In the context of a pilot facing the fear of failure, a CBT therapist would help the pilot identify negative thought patterns related to the fear of failure, such as "If I fail, I'll never be able to fly again" or "If I fail, everyone will think I'm a bad pilot". These thoughts can be challenged and replaced with more realistic and positive thoughts, such as "Failing doesn't mean I can never fly again. It just means I need to work on improving my skills" or "Everyone makes mistakes. Failing doesn't make me a bad pilot".

The therapist may also work with the pilot on relaxation techniques to help reduce physical symptoms of stress, such as deep breathing exercises, progressive muscle relaxation, or meditation. Additionally, the therapist may work with the pilot to develop coping strategies for stress, such as breaking down tasks into smaller, manageable steps, or focusing on the present moment rather than worrying about the future. This can help pilots facing the fear of failure to reframe their negative thought patterns, reduce physical symptoms of stress, and develop coping strategies to improve their resilience. In such cases seek support from trusted colleagues or mental health professionals if needed and develop a plan for accessing resources and support when necessary.

By applying these strategies, flight crews can better cope with the demands of the profession.

A. Understanding resilience and its impact on wellbeing. Resilience refers to the ability to bounce back from challenges and adversity. Maintaining resilience is crucial to maintaining overall wellbeing, as it allows individuals to effectively manage stress and overcome obstacles. The impact of resilience on wellbeing can be seen in improved physical health, increased positive emotions, and reduced stress and anxiety.

B. Building physical and mental resilience. There are several ways that flight crews can build physical and mental resilience. Physical resilience can be built through regular exercise, proper nutrition, and adequate rest and recovery. Mental resilience can be built through practices such as meditation, positive thinking, and the methods and techniques outlined in this Top Mind system of mental training.

C. The role of positive thinking and meditation. Positive thinking and meditation are powerful tools for building resilience and maintaining wellbeing.

Examples of how flight crews can apply these lessons.

A. Self-awareness. Flight crews can cultivate self-awareness by regularly checking in with themselves and taking note of their emotional and physical states. This can involve practices such as journaling or meditation, or simply taking a few minutes each day to reflect on how you are feeling.

B. Identifying triggers and sources of stress. You can identify triggers and sources of stress by paying attention to the situations and circumstances that tend to cause you to feel overwhelmed or anxious. This can involve keeping a journal of stressful situations or taking note of patterns in your mood or behavior.

C. Lifestyle factors that impact wellbeing/ You can improve your wellbeing by focusing on lifestyle factors such as nutrition, exercise, and sleep. This might involve setting aside time each day for physical activity, making healthy food choices while on the job, or establishing a regular sleep schedule.

D. Coping strategies for stress and anxiety. Develop coping strategies for stress and anxiety by practicing meditation, engaging in relaxation techniques such as deep breathing or progressive muscle relaxation, or seeking support from colleagues, family, or mental health professionals.

Relationship Management Skills Contribute to Wellbeing.

Relationship management is one of the key components of emotional intelligence, and it refers to the ability to build and maintain positive relationships with others. In the context of aviation, pilots and crew with strong relationship management skills are better able to collaborate with colleagues, communicate effectively with air traffic controllers, and manage interactions with passengers. The same skills are vital for astronauts who must work in isolated confined spaces for long periods of time.

Here are some examples of relationship management skills that are particularly valuable for pilots and astronauts,

- Effective communication. Pilots with strong relationship management skills can communicate clearly and effectively with others. They listen actively to others, express their own ideas and feelings clearly, and seek to find common ground with others. Astronauts must be able to communicate effectively with each other, mission control, and scientists on the ground. They must be able to convey complex information clearly and concisely, and they must be able to listen actively to others to ensure that they understand their needs and concerns.
- Conflict resolution. Pilots and astronauts with strong relationship management skills manage conflicts effectively when they arise. They listen to the perspectives of others, seek to find common ground, and work collaboratively to find solutions that meet everyone's needs.
- Collaboration. Pilots and astronauts with strong relationship management skills can work effectively with others to achieve common goals. They build and maintain positive relationships

with colleagues, air traffic controllers, and passengers, and they are able to work collaboratively to find creative solutions to complex problems.

- Empathy. Pilots with strong relationship management skills can understand and relate to the emotions of others. They see situations from multiple perspectives and respond in a way that is compassionate and understanding.
- Influence. Pilots with strong relationship management skills influence others in a positive way. They can inspire and motivate others, and they are able to use their interpersonal skills to achieve positive outcomes.

Furthermore, the unique environment of space can create additional challenges for relationship management. Astronauts are in a confined space for long periods of time, and they may experience isolation, homesickness, and other emotional stresses. This can make effective communication and collaboration even more important.

In addition, space missions often involve international collaboration, with astronauts from different countries working together towards a common goal. This can create additional challenges in terms of language barriers, cultural differences, and different communication styles. Effective relationship management skills can help astronauts navigate these challenges and build positive relationships with their international colleagues.

Relationship management skills can also be important for maintaining positive relationships with loved ones back on Earth. Astronauts may experience long periods of separation from their families and friends, and effective communication and empathy can help to maintain these relationships and provide support during the mission.

Here are some tips and hacks for developing relationship management skills as an astronaut:

1. Practice active listening. Active listening is an essential component of effective communication and conflict resolution. To practice active listening, make a conscious effort to focus on what the other person is saying, ask clarifying questions, and summarize what they've said to ensure that you understand their perspective.
2. Learn about other cultures. When working with international colleagues, take the time to learn about their culture and communication style. This can help you to build positive relationships and avoid misunderstandings.
3. Develop emotional intelligence. Emotional intelligence is the foundation of relationship management skills. Practice self-awareness, self-regulation, empathy, and social skills to develop your emotional intelligence and improve your ability to manage relationships.
4. Use nonverbal communication. Nonverbal communication can be just as important as verbal communication, especially in a confined space. Use body language, facial expressions, and other nonverbal cues to convey your thoughts and feelings and to build rapport with others.
5. Take breaks. Spending long periods of time in a confined space can be emotionally challenging. Take breaks when you need to and find ways to recharge and take care of yourself.
6. Use technology to stay connected. Technology can be a valuable tool for maintaining relationships with loved ones back on Earth. Use video calls, messaging apps, and other tools to stay connected with family and friends.
7. Practice conflict resolution. Conflict is inevitable in any group setting, especially when spending long periods of time in a confined space. Practice conflict resolution techniques such as active listening, seeking common ground, and finding creative solutions to problems.

Zen

Zen is a philosophy and practice that can help you find inner peace and alleviate stress and anxiety. One of the core teachings of Zen is being fully present in the moment. In your line of work, being present and focused is crucial for safety. When you are flying, try to let go of any distractions or worries and focus completely on the task at hand. Pay attention to your breath and your surroundings, and let your mind be still.

A principle in Zen is the idea of letting go of attachments and expectations. In your job, you may experience a lot of pressure to perform perfectly. This can create unnecessary tension and anxiety. Instead of clinging to expectations and outcomes, try to let go of them and focus on the process. Trust in your training and your abilities and stay present in the moment.

In Zen, meditation is a key practice for cultivating inner peace. You can incorporate meditation into your daily routine by taking a few moments to sit quietly and focus on your breath. Even just a few minutes of daily meditation can help reduce stress.

Zen also focusses on the qualities of compassion and empathy. As flight crew, you can serve and help others. Cultivating compassion and empathy will help you connect with your passengers and create a more positive and peaceful atmosphere on board. Zen is not just a practice, but a way of life. Incorporating Zen principles into your daily routines, thoughts, and actions can help you find greater peace and fulfillment in all aspects of your life, both on and off the plane.

In the case of aerospace professionals and astronauts, as space explorers, you experience unique challenges. Isolation, confinement, and uncertainty can take a toll on your physical and mental wellbeing. Zen can offer a valuable approach to help you navigate these challenges and cultivate a sense of inner peace and calm. An aspect of Zen that may also benefit you is the principle of non-attachment. This involves recognizing that everything is impermanent and letting go of our attachment to specific outcomes or experiences. In the context of space exploration, this may mean accepting the inherent risks and uncertainties and focusing on the present moment rather than worrying about the risks. As astronauts, you are part of a larger community working towards a common goal. Practicing Zen philosophy and compassion towards yourself and others can help you navigate the challenges of space exploration and cultivate a sense of connection and support. Incorporating Zen into your life may take time and practice, but with dedication, it can offer valuable tools for navigating the challenges of space exploration and cultivating resilience and excellence. The practice of Zen involves emphasizes rigorous self-control, meditation and other contemplative techniques aimed at cultivating inner peace, insight, and wisdom, and ultimately leading to the experience of enlightenment or realization of one's true nature. Zen is also characterized by a direct and intuitive approach to spiritual practice, emphasizing the experience of the present moment and the importance of letting go of conceptual thinking and intellectual analysis.

Zazen exercise

As mentioned earlier in the section on Samurai, one fundamental practice in Zen that you as professionals can apply is zazen or sitting meditation. Zazen involves sitting still and focusing on the breath, in some practices you may mentally repeat a phrase or mantra, bringing awareness to the present moment and letting go of distracting thoughts.

Here are some examples of how you can incorporate zazen into your life:

- Before a flight. Taking a few minutes to sit in zazen can help you clear your mind and reduce any pre-flight jitters or anxiety.
- During a break. When you have some downtime, they can take a few minutes to sit in zazen, helping them to recharge and stay focused.
- In moments of stress. If a stressful situation arises during a flight or mission, you can take a few deep breaths and practice zazen to help you regain focus and composure.
- When dealing with jet lag. Zazen can also help the flight crew adjust to time zone changes and overcome the effects of jet lag by promoting relaxation and reducing stress.

Through regular practice of zazen, you can develop a greater sense of mental clarity, focus, and inner peace, which can improve your overall performance.

Native American and Indigenous Wisdom

I'd like to share with you some insights from Native American and indigenous traditions that I believe can help you cultivate courage, confidence, and poise in your work. One of the key teachings of these traditions is the importance of connection – connection to the earth, to each other, and to our own inner wisdom. When we are disconnected, we feel lost, alone, and afraid. When we are connected, we feel grounded, supported, and empowered. Native American and indigenous peoples have always had a deep understanding of the interconnectedness of all things in the universe.

Many indigenous peoples believe that everyone has a unique purpose in life, a sacred mission that they must fulfill. Reflect on your own purpose and mission and by connecting with this purpose, you will tap into a deep reservoir of courage and strength. This means recognizing the interdependence of your roles and responsibilities. Each of you has a unique contribution to make, and when you work together with your teams in harmony, you create a powerful force for good results.

In the Native American tradition, courage is not the absence of fear, but the willingness to face our fears and overcome them. You may face challenges and obstacles but know that you have the strength and resilience within you to meet them head-on. Trust in your own inner wisdom and your connection to each other and to the earth. You are part of a greater whole, and you are supported by the wisdom and traditions of those who have come before you. Trust in your own inner strength and stay connected to each other, the universe and to the earth.

A meteor's color is determined by the chemical elements and compounds that make it up. Similarly, the color of our life, or rather the quality of our life, is determined by our mental composition, which includes our thoughts, attitudes, beliefs, and emotions.

Our mental composition is shaped by our experiences, upbringing, education, and other factors. If we have a positive mental composition, our life can be full of vibrant colors, much like a meteor that is composed of colorful elements. On the other hand, if our mental composition is negative, our life can be dull and monochromatic.

To improve the quality of our lives, we can work on improving our mental composition through mind training. We can shift our mental composition towards more positive and uplifting states, which can lead to a more fulfilling and colorful life.

Just as the chemical composition of a meteor can be analyzed to reveal its origin and history, we can also examine our mental composition to understand our past experiences and how they have shaped us. If an individual has a positive and optimistic mindset, they are more likely to experience their life in a positive light. On the other hand, if they have a negative and pessimistic mindset, their experiences may be colored with negativity. Just like a meteor's color reveals its chemical composition, an individual's mental composition reveals their inner world and the lens through which they perceive their reality.

Getting Out of Your Own Way
The Unconscious Mind

The unconscious mind is the storehouse of your creativity, your intuition, your emotions, your memories, and your instincts. It is a vast reservoir of resources that you can tap into to achieve your goals and dreams.

Harnessing the power of your unconscious mind is aided by getting out of your own way and learning how to pass through the threshold of consciousness by a process of focus and relaxation you can allow the unconscious to perform in a flow state of ease, where you are feeling the movement rather than thinking about it. You need to let go of the limiting beliefs, negative self-talk, and self-doubt that are holding you back.

Have faith in yourself and your abilities. You must trust that you have the capacity to overcome obstacles and achieve the aims you set your mind to.

Create a fertile environment for your unconscious mind to thrive. This means taking care of your physical, mental, and emotional well-being. You must eat nutritious foods, get plenty of rest, exercise regularly, and manage your stress levels. You must also engage in activities that bring you joy and fulfillment, such as hobbies, creative pursuits, and meaningful relationships. Nourish humor and joy and bliss on a regular basis. Cultivate a receptive mindset that allows your unconscious mind to communicate with your conscious mind. Be open to new experiences, ideas, and perspectives. It means being curious, imaginative, and non-judgmental. It means paying attention to your dreams, your intuition, and your gut feelings. It means trusting the process and being patient. Learn to connect and trust this inner level of mind. You can tap into the vast resources of your unconscious mind and unleash your true potential. All you have to do is get out of your own way, create a fertile environment, and cultivate a receptive mindset.

The unconscious mind in shaping our thoughts and behaviors. The unconscious mind is the repository of our past experiences, memories, and emotions that we are not aware of in our conscious mind. It influences our conscious mind in subtle ways, affecting our decisions, behaviors, and emotional responses. To harness the power of the unconscious mind, it's important to understand its workings and how it affects our conscious mind. By becoming more aware of our thoughts, emotions, and behaviors, we can start to identify patterns and triggers that are rooted in the unconscious mind.

You may not realize it, but your unconscious mind is responsible for much of what you do and achieve in life. It's where your deepest desires and motivations reside, and it's also where your greatest fears and doubts hide. One of the keys to utilizing the power of your unconscious mind is to understand that it is always working behind the scenes. It's constantly processing information and making connections that you may not even be aware of. By tapping into this wealth of knowledge and intuition, you can gain insights and ideas that you may not have otherwise thought of. Getting out of your own way is about learning to let go of conscious control. Often, we try to control every aspect of our lives and force ourselves to think and act in a certain way. This can limit our potential and prevent us from tapping into the vast resources of our unconscious mind. By learning to relax and let go of control, you can allow your unconscious mind to take the lead and guide you towards the best possible outcomes.

Visualization while in a relaxed state is a way to tap into the power of your unconscious mind. By creating vivid mental images of what you want to achieve, you can program your unconscious mind to work towards those goals. This is because the unconscious mind cannot distinguish between what is real and what is imagined. By visualizing your desired outcomes, you are essentially programming your mind to work towards making them a reality.

The unconscious mind is deeply interconnected with the rest of your being. When taking care of your physical, emotional, and spiritual health, you are also nurturing your unconscious mind. Make sure to take care of yourself in all aspects of your life, and your unconscious mind will reward you accordingly. The problem is that we often get in our own way. We let our conscious mind, with its doubts and fears, override our unconscious mind. We tell ourselves that we're not good enough or that we can't do something, and that blocks the flow of our natural abilities and talents.

Here's the thing, if we can learn to get out of our own way, if we can learn to quiet our conscious mind and allow our unconscious mind to take over, we can tap into a whole world of potential and creativity. We need to recognize when we're telling ourselves that we can't do something or that we're not good enough. Once we're aware of those thoughts, we can start to challenge them and replace them with more positive and empowering beliefs. Relax and allow your imagination to come through. Our bodies are incredibly sophisticated, and the unconscious mind plays a critical role in ensuring that we operate efficiently and effectively.

When it comes to flying, there are a multitude of physiological responses that occur unconsciously within the body. These responses can have a significant impact on performance. For example, when faced with a sudden emergency or dangerous situation, the body's stress response is activated, releasing adrenaline and other hormones into the bloodstream. This can result in heightened alertness and reaction times, which can be essential in the event of a crisis.

However, prolonged exposure to stress and anxiety can have negative effects on performance, leading to reduced attention and concentration, impaired decision-making abilities, and increased fatigue. This is where the power of the unconscious mind comes in.

By tapping into the unconscious mind, we can learn to regulate our physiological responses and manage stress and anxiety more effectively. Techniques such as deep breathing, visualization, and mindfulness meditation can all help to activate the body's relaxation response, which counteracts the effects of the stress response. For example, before a flight, you might take a few moments to close your eyes and focus on your breath. As you inhale, imagine calm, peaceful thoughts and sensations flowing through your body. As you exhale, imagine tension and stress leaving your body. With practice, you can train your body to activate the relaxation response on demand, helping you to stay calm and focused even in stressful situations.

For the Flight Deck Crew as you continue to hone your skills and become more experienced pilots, you'll likely find that much of what you do in the cockpit becomes automatic. That's the unconscious mind at work. But it's not just about muscle memory and habits. The unconscious mind also plays a role in decision making, problem solving, and even in managing stress.

Let's say you're faced with an emergency in flight. Your conscious mind is likely to be overwhelmed by the suddenness and severity of the situation. Your unconscious mind, drawing on your training and experience, can quickly evaluate the options and come up with a plan of action. In this way, the unconscious mind can help you make split-second decisions that can mean the difference between life and death.

On the other hand, if you're feeling anxious or stressed before a flight, that too can impact your performance. Negative thoughts and emotions can activate the sympathetic nervous system, leading to an increase in heart rate, breathing rate, and blood pressure. This can impair your ability to concentrate, react quickly, and make sound decisions.

By learning to tap into the power of your unconscious mind, you can not only improve your performance in the cockpit but also manage stress and anxiety more effectively. One technique that can help is visualization. By visualizing yourself successfully executing a flight or maneuver, you can program your unconscious mind to help make it a reality. I've known some pilots who would simulate and visualize full flights segments in their bed before important Line check rides for example, the pilot called it flying the bed. The concept is the same. You can also use relaxation techniques like deep breathing and progressive muscle relaxation to calm the sympathetic nervous system and reduce stress.

The unconscious mind is a powerful part of your mind that can work for you or against you. Learning to harness its power, you can take your flying to the next level and achieve your goals with confidence and ease.

The conscious mind can be likened to the captain of an aircraft, responsible for setting the course and making decisions based on the information available to them. But just as the captain relies on the systems and instruments of the aircraft to provide them with crucial information, so too does the conscious mind rely on the unconscious processes of the brain to provide it with the information it needs to make decisions and perform effectively. Think of it this way, the conscious mind is like the tip of an iceberg, visible above the surface of the water, but representing only a small fraction of the whole. Beneath the surface lies the vast bulk of the iceberg, representing the unconscious processes that drive our thoughts, feelings, and behaviors. When you are flying, for example, your conscious mind may be focused on navigating the plane, communicating with air traffic control, and making decisions about course corrections. However, beneath the surface, our unconscious mind is also at work, monitoring the plane's instruments, responding to changes in air pressure and turbulence, and providing us with intuitive hunches or insights that may help us make better decisions.

I'd also like to point out that the conscious and unconscious mind are not truly separate entities, but rather two complementary aspects of the same system. By learning to work with both the conscious and unconscious mind, we can tap into the full power of our brains and achieve optimal performance in any situation. Harmonious coordination between these two phases of your mind is essential for top performance. Imagine a pilot who is performing a complex maneuver such as landing in difficult weather conditions. The conscious mind is like the pilot in the cockpit, making decisions, controlling the plane's movements, and communicating with the control tower. But the unconscious mind is like the autopilot system, constantly monitoring the plane's systems, adjusting the engines and wings, and making sure everything is running smoothly. Imagine if the pilot were to ignore the unconscious processes and try to control everything consciously. They would become overwhelmed, stressed, and their performance would suffer. The same is true in our everyday lives. If we try to control everything consciously, we become overwhelmed and stressed, and our performance suffers.

If we trust in the unconscious processes and allow them to work in harmony with our conscious decisions, we can achieve a state of flow and peak performance. This is the essence of utilizing the full potential of our mind, and it applies not only to flying but also to all aspects of life.

Here are some techniques to help you achieve a state of flow and peak performance, where the conscious and unconscious mind work in harmony.

It's essential to set clear goals and have a deep understanding of the task at hand. This helps the conscious and unconscious mind to work together towards a common goal or mission objective.

Secondly, it's crucial to be fully present and immersed in the task at hand, letting go of any distractions and unnecessary thoughts. This allows the unconscious mind to take over and perform at its best.

Practice and repetition are key. The more you train your conscious and unconscious mind to work together towards a specific task, the more you'll be able to achieve a state of flow and peak performance.

It's essential to trust your unconscious mind and let it do its job. The unconscious mind is like a powerful machine, and once you've set clear goals and practiced, it will do its job and lead you towards success. The conscious and unconscious mind are like the captain and aircraft, working together towards a common goal. Trust in yourself and your abilities, and you'll be able to achieve greatness. Trust in your abilities is about faith and belief. By relaxing your conscious mind and allowing your unconscious to take over, you can tap into a deeper level of awareness and unlock your full potential. It is also important to promote a sense of faith in the process. Believe your unconscious mind is working for you, even when you are not consciously aware of it. This sense of faith can help you stay calm and centered in challenging situations, allowing you to perform at your best.

The unconscious mind is a powerful ally and has been honed by evolution over thousands of years to help us survive and thrive. By learning to trust and harness its power, you can achieve greater levels of success and fulfillment in all areas of your life.

Trusting the unconscious mind and allowing it to work for you is not the same as being passive. You still need to actively engage in your *training, practice, and preparation*. But it is about allowing your natural abilities and skills to flow through you effortlessly, without the interference of doubt, fear, or overthinking.

Think of a professional tennis player. They train for hours and hours, perfecting their form, technique, and strategy. However, during a match, they cannot afford to be constantly thinking about their movements or doubting their abilities. They need to trust in their unconscious mind to execute the shots they have practiced so many times. When they are in the zone, or in a state of flow, everything seems to come naturally, without conscious effort.

Trust in it, prepare for it, and allow it to work for you. You are not alone in the cockpit, your unconscious mind is like another co-pilot, and when you work together in harmony, you can achieve peak performance and excel in your flying career. I have seen this happen time and time again in my own life and in the lives of those I have worked with. When you trust in your unconscious processes and allow yourself to enter a state of flow, you will be amazed at what you can accomplish.

Belief Systems

Beliefs are formed through a combination of conscious and unconscious processes. Our conscious mind evaluates incoming information and decides whether to accept it. If we accept the information, it becomes part of our belief system. However, there are also unconscious processes that contribute to the formation of our beliefs. These unconscious processes are influenced by our experiences, our emotions, and our environment. If we have a traumatic experience, our unconscious mind may form a belief that similar situations are dangerous and should be avoided. Similarly, if we are raised in a certain cultural or religious environment, our unconscious mind may form beliefs that are consistent with those values.

Beliefs influence our behavior and our perceptions of the world around us. If we hold a belief that something is true, we may be more likely to interpret information in a way that supports that belief. This can be both positive and negative, depending on the nature of the belief. By understanding the way beliefs are formed, we can work to change them if they are limiting our potential or causing us to view the world in a negative way. By identifying limiting beliefs and working to change them, you can open new possibilities for growth. Belief systems are constructed over time through repeated experiences and the meanings we assign to those experiences. These beliefs then shape our thoughts, emotions, and actions, creating a self-fulfilling cycle.

The good news is that these belief systems can be changed through the power of suggestion and positive affirmations. By repeating positive statements to yourself and visualizing the outcomes you desire, you can reprogram your unconscious mind to support your goals and aspirations. For example, if you have a belief that you are not good enough or not skilled enough to perform a particular task, this negative belief will likely manifest in your thoughts and actions, leading to a self-fulfilling prophecy of failure. But if you begin to consciously focus on positive affirmations and visualize yourself successfully completing the task, you can begin to shift your belief system and tap into the power of your unconscious mind to achieve your goals.

Take some time to reflect on your beliefs and thought patterns and begin to consciously shift them towards positivity and success. With consistent practice and dedication, you will learn to tap into the power of your unconscious to greater degrees.

Self-Image

Our beliefs and self-image can either limit or enhance our abilities. In essence, the mind is like a computer, and our beliefs are the programs that we run. If we have negative beliefs about ourselves, we will limit our potential and hinder our progress. Conversely, if we have positive beliefs, we can achieve great things and overcome any obstacles in our way. I want to share with you the concept of self-image. Our self-image is the mental picture we have of ourselves, and it determines how we think, feel, and behave. If we see ourselves as confident and capable individuals, we will act accordingly and achieve success. On the other hand, if we see ourselves as inadequate and unworthy, we will struggle to achieve our goals. We have the power to change our self-image and create a new reality for ourselves. Through visualization and mental rehearsal, we can program our minds to see ourselves in a positive light and achieve our full potential. This is the foundation of the concept of creative visualization, which has been used by athletes, business leaders, aviation and aerospace professionals to achieve peak performance.

Take a close look at your self-image and ask yourself if it is serving you or limiting you. If it is the latter, know that you have the power to change it and create a new reality for yourself. I believe that by changing our self-image, we can significantly alter our experience of life.

How can this be applied to cabin crews? As you know, your job can be demanding and stressful at times. Try to remember that you can handle any situation that comes your way. Your mind is a powerful tool that can either help or hinder your performance.

Imagine you're on a flight and you encounter turbulence. Your first instinct may be to panic or become anxious. However, if you can shift your mindset and believe that you are a skilled and experienced cabin crew member who is fully capable of handling the situation, you are more likely to remain calm and focused.

You see, your beliefs and self-image have a direct impact on your performance. If you believe that you are a competent and confident cabin crew member, you will act accordingly. On the contrary if you doubt yourself or let fear take over, your performance may suffer. In other words, it relates to your self-confidence.

My recommendation is to take a few moments before each flight to visualize yourself performing at your best. See yourself confidently handling any situation that arises. Believe in yourself and your abilities. This habit and process will help you tap into the power of your mind and achieve peak performance.

Happiness

When we think of happiness, we often think of it as a state of mind that's difficult to attain, like it's some far-off destination that we need to work hard to get to. The truth is, happiness isn't a destination, it's a journey. It's something that we can cultivate and nurture within ourselves every day. The first step to finding happiness is to accept that it's not something that we can buy or achieve through external means. Happiness comes from within, from a sense of contentment and fulfillment that we create within ourselves. One way to cultivate happiness is to focus on gratitude. Take a moment every day to reflect on the things that you're grateful for, whether it's a kind gesture from a colleague, a beautiful sunset, or a delicious meal. Gratitude helps us to shift our focus from what we lack to what we have, and it opens our hearts to the abundance and beauty of life. Another way to find happiness is to practice kindness. When we do something kind for someone else, we experience a sense of warmth and joy that's difficult to replicate through any other means. It doesn't have to be a grand gesture – a simple smile or a compliment can brighten someone's day and create a ripple effect of positivity.

Appreciate the beauty and richness of our daily experiences fully engage with our surroundings, whether it's the taste of our food, the feel of the breeze on our skin, or the sound of a loved one's voice. Happiness means different things to different people. For some, it may be achieving a certain level of success in their careers, while for others it may be having strong relationships or being able to pursue their passions.

It's so easy to get caught up in the stress and negativity of our daily lives, but taking time to appreciate the things we have can help us feel more fulfilled and content. Try starting a gratitude journal, where you write down three things, you're grateful for each day. It can be as simple as having a roof over your head or enjoying a good meal, but taking a moment to acknowledge these things can shift your focus to the positive.

Happiness is finding meaning and purpose in your life. This can come from a variety of sources - your work, your relationships, your hobbies - but it's important to have something that gives you a sense of fulfillment and satisfaction. Ask yourself, what do you value most in life? What motivates you? What makes you feel like you're making a difference in the world? Once you have a sense of what's truly important to you, make it a priority in your life.

It's easy to neglect our own well-being when we're focused on other things, but taking care of ourselves is essential for our overall happiness. This means getting enough sleep, eating well, and exercising regularly. It also means setting boundaries and taking time for activities that recharge you, whether that's reading a book, spending time with loved ones, or pursuing a hobby. You can't pour from an empty cup - taking care of yourself allows you to show up fully in your life and for the people around you.

Happiness is not something that happens to us, but something we create for ourselves. happiness is not something that can be obtained overnight or through material possessions. It is a state of mind that needs to be cultivated through our thoughts and actions. Let me give you an example.

Imagine you are a pilot flying a plane through a storm. You are doing everything in your power to navigate through the turbulence and bring the plane to safety. At that moment you are fully present, you are not concerned with the latest gadgets or luxury items, but solely focused on the task at hand. Despite the difficult circumstances, you are in a state of flow, and your mind is fully engaged in the present moment.

Now imagine that same pilot off duty, worrying about his financial status or feeling unfulfilled in his personal life. These negative thoughts create a sense of unhappiness, even though he may have all the material possessions that he or she desires.

This example illustrates the power of the mind and the impact our thoughts have on our emotions. By focusing on the present moment and being fully engaged in our actions, we can cultivate a state of flow and happiness, even in challenging circumstances.

As I mentioned earlier you can cultivate happiness through acts of kindness and service to others. When we help others, it not only benefits them but also brings us a sense of fulfillment and joy. This can be as simple as holding the door open for someone or volunteering at a local charity or complimenting your colleagues on a job well done. Just as a negative criticism can throw us off for a long time, a compliment can do wonders to bring about joy in a person's day. I do not refer to false flattery or anything like that, but rather giving credit where credit is due and not hesitating to provide a compliment where it is merited.

Whether we are pilots, cabin crew members, engineers, or consultants, we all have a duty to fulfill. With these duties come challenges that can make us feel overwhelmed or powerless. Our ability to overcome these challenges lies not in external circumstances but within ourselves. It is our mindset that shapes our perception and determines our actions. Try to develop a mindset that is grounded in reason and virtue. This means understanding that the only things within our control are our thoughts, actions, and attitudes. Everything else is outside of our control, and it is pointless to worry about such things.

In moments of stress or frustration, it is easy to become reactive and lose sight of what truly matters. This is where the practice of self-reflection comes in. By taking a step back and observing our thoughts and emotions, we can gain greater clarity and make more intentional decisions. We should strive to be kind, just, and compassionate in our interactions with others, even in the face of adversity.

Stoic Ideas Applied

As astronauts and flight crews, and ground and ATC professionals you face unique challenges and must possess and develop exceptional qualities to succeed in your work. I want to share with you some Stoic philosophy insights on the principles of courage (in section three), discipline, justice, and wisdom that can help you in your approach to your careers and life in general.

Stoic Idea of Justice

Justice is also an important principle that you should strive to embody in your work and life. Justice is about treating others with fairness, respect, and compassion. As astronauts and flight crews, you work in a highly interdependent and collaborative environment, and it's essential that you treat each other with the utmost respect and consideration. Justice is not just about following rules and laws; it's about acting with integrity, empathy, and compassion.

Justice is an important aspect of any profession. It means doing what is right and fair, not just for us but also for others. In aviation and aerospace industries, justice is crucial as it affects the safety of passengers, crew, and equipment.

As professionals in this field, we have a duty to uphold justice in all aspects of our work. We must ensure that we are following all safety protocols and regulations, treating all passengers and crew members with respect and dignity, and addressing any issues or concerns in a fair and just manner.

In order to achieve justice in our work, we must first develop a strong sense of personal integrity. This means being honest and transparent in all our actions and decisions. We must also develop a strong sense of empathy and compassion for others, so that we can understand their perspectives and needs and respond accordingly. It's about creating a safe, fair, and equitable environment for all. We each have a responsibility to ensure that justice is upheld in all aspects of our work, so that we can build trust with our colleagues, customers, and stakeholders.

Stoic Idea of Wisdom

Wisdom is the ability to see beyond appearances, to understand the deeper patterns and principles that govern our world, and to make wise decisions based on that understanding. Wisdom requires humility, curiosity, and a willingness to learn from experience. You develop your wisdom by seeking out diverse perspectives, reflecting on your experiences, and pursuing a lifelong journey of learning and growth.

Wisdom is often associated with age and experience, but it goes beyond that. It is the ability to use knowledge, experience, and insight to make sound judgments and decisions. Wisdom is about knowing what to do in any given situation and doing it in a way that is not only beneficial to you, but also to those around you.

These principles are not just abstract ideals; they are practical tools that can help you navigate the challenges and uncertainties of your work and achieve your goals.

Confidence, Serenity and an Earnest Desire

Your mental state plays a critical role in your professional performance focus. Having faith and confidence in one's abilities is essential for perfect focus. By using autosuggestion, the subjective mind can be charged with faith and confidence. Even if your objective belief does not match the subjective impression, the latter will obtain control unconsciously to the subjective unconscious mind, and the desired outcome will be achieved. This last sentence contains a mark of wisdom that should not be overlooked. It contains the mechanism by which many of our automatic emotional triggers can be set.

The power to achieve optimum focus is within reach. However, you must be willing to get into the correct state of mind and possess the requisite mental equilibrium to become sufficiently serene, relaxed and calm. Confidence can be commanded through autosuggestion, even in the presence of objective unbelief. A calm serenity of mind is indispensable for achieving the desired results. To exercise peak performance focus, three ingredients are beneficial: confidence, a calm serenity of mind, and an earnest desire to bring about the results.

Be Adaptable

The remote volcanic Galapagos Islands, located in the Pacific Ocean, are home to a unique array of species, many of which are found nowhere else on Earth. The Galapagos are known for their role in the development of Charles Darwin's theory of evolution by natural selection. What I find remarkable about this is how it illustrates the power of adaptation. You see, the animals and plants that live on the Galapagos Islands have had to adapt to a harsh and unpredictable environment, where resources are limited, and the conditions are constantly changing. Those species that were able to adapt the fastest, and most effectively, were the ones that survived and thrived.

Now, what does this have to do with you? I believe that the principle of adaptation is just as relevant to us as it is to the animals and plants of the Galapagos Islands. In our rapidly changing world, we must be able to adapt to new situations, new challenges, and new opportunities. Those of us who can do so most effectively are the ones who will succeed. Be willing to learn, to grow, and to change. Embrace new ideas, new technologies, and new ways of doing things. Always be ready to adjust your approach when the situation demands it. Evolution is an ongoing process, happening all around us, all the time. If we can harness the power of adaptation, we too can thrive in this ever-changing world. Airline business models change over time and the ones that did not make it were the ones that did not adopt quick enough.

In order to adapt, one must be open and flexible to change. Innovation and creative thinking are vital skills in an ever-changing world. This is where practical tools come into play. One such tool is the ability to assess and analyze situations objectively. By taking a step back and looking at the bigger picture, we can see things more clearly and make informed decisions. It's the view from different flight levels and other perspectives, the 30000 feet perspective is very different to ground level. The ability to be resilient in the face of adversity is also a useful trait. There will undoubtedly be obstacles along the way, but it's how we respond to those obstacles that truly matters. By maintaining a positive attitude and finding ways to overcome challenges, we can build our resilience and become even more adaptable. Perhaps the most important tool for adaptation is learning. Constantly seeking out new knowledge and experiences can expand our understanding of the world and improve our ability to adapt to change. This could mean taking on new challenges, exploring new interests, or simply being open to learning from others. Now, let me give you an example that is relevant to your profession. In the aviation industry, changes happen rapidly and unexpectedly. As a pilot, you must be able to adapt to changing weather conditions, new technology, and new aircraft designs and systems, technical malfunctions, and potentially other unforeseen circumstances. Using the tools of objective analysis, resilience, and learning, you can become more adaptable and effective in your role. Be open to change, to stay positive in the face of adversity, and to always keep learning. Initiative, imagination and innovation are important skills when operating in a constantly changing dynamic environment.

Sleep Hygiene

Sleep hygiene refers to a set of practices that are aimed at promoting good quality sleep and reducing the risk of sleep-related problems. Poor sleep hygiene has been associated with a range of negative outcomes, including increased stress, reduced cognitive performance, and an increased risk of developing chronic diseases. In this section, we will explore the importance of good sleep hygiene, and provide some tips and strategies for improving your sleep habits.

Why Is Good Sleep Hygiene Important?

Sleep is essential for our physical and mental health, and poor-quality sleep can have a negative impact on our overall wellbeing. Lack of sleep has been linked to a range of health problems, including obesity, diabetes, cardiovascular disease, and mental health problems such as depression and anxiety.

Good sleep hygiene is important for several reasons. Firstly, it helps to ensure that you get enough sleep each night. Most adults need between 7-9 hours of sleep each night, but many people fail to achieve this due to poor sleep habits. By practicing good sleep hygiene, you can help to ensure that you get the recommended amount of sleep each night, which can have numerous benefits for your physical and mental health.

In addition to promoting good sleep quantity, good sleep hygiene is also important for ensuring good sleep quality. Poor sleep hygiene can lead to disrupted sleep, frequent awakenings, and shallow sleep. This can leave you feeling tired and groggy the next day and can impair your cognitive and physical performance. By practicing good sleep hygiene, you can help to ensure that you get deep, restorative sleep each night, which can help you to feel more alert and energized during the day.

Tips for Improving Your Sleep Hygiene

How can you improve your sleep hygiene? Here are some tips and strategies that you can try:

- Stick to a regular sleep schedule. Try to go to bed and wake up at the same time each day, even on weekends. This helps to regulate your body clock and can improve your sleep quality.
- Create a relaxing bedtime routine. Establish a regular routine that you follow each night before bed. This could include taking a warm bath, reading a book, or practicing relaxation techniques such as deep breathing or meditation.
- Make your bedroom a sleep-friendly environment. Your bedroom should be cool, dark, and quiet. Invest in comfortable mattresses and pillows, and remove any distractions such as TVs, computers, or bright lights.
- Limit your exposure to screens before bed. The blue light emitted by electronic devices such as smartphones and tablets can interfere with your body clock and disrupt your sleep. Try to avoid using these devices for at least an hour before bed.
- Avoid caffeine and alcohol before bed. Caffeine is a stimulant that can make it difficult to fall asleep, while alcohol can disrupt your sleep and lead to frequent awakenings.
- Regular exercise can improve your sleep quality and duration. However, it is important to avoid exercising too close to bedtime, as this can make it difficult to fall asleep.
- Stress and anxiety can interfere with your sleep. Practice stress-reduction techniques such as mindfulness, yoga, or deep breathing to help you relax and unwind before bed.

Good sleep hygiene is essential for maintaining good physical and mental health. By practicing good sleep habits, you can help to ensure that you get enough high-quality sleep each night, which can have numerous benefits for your wellbeing.

As you know, the aviation and aerospace industries require a high level of performance and attention to detail. The consequences of a mistake can be very serious indeed. Therefore, it is critical that you prioritize your sleep and make sure you are well-rested before performing any tasks related to your work.

Research has shown that fatigue is a risk factor in aviation accidents. In addition, the Federal Aviation Administration has implemented regulations aimed at ensuring that pilots and other aviation personnel are not fatigued while on duty. These regulations include limits on the number of hours a pilot can fly in a day or week, as well as mandatory rest periods.

As you may know, flying an aircraft is a complex and demanding task that requires a high level of alertness and focus. That's why it's essential for flight crews to get enough rest and sleep to maintain their mental and physical health.

The aviation industry has recognized the importance of rest time, and there are specific regulations and guidelines that airlines must follow to ensure their flight crews have adequate rest periods. In the United States, the Federal Aviation Administration (FAA) mandates the minimum rest requirements for flight crews.

According to the FAA regulations, flight crews must have at least 10 hours of rest between duty periods. The rest period should include a continuous period of at least 8 hours of sleep opportunity at the crew member's designated sleep period, with an additional 2 hours of rest or sleep opportunity. Furthermore, the maximum flight duty period is generally limited to 14 hours.

These rest time requirements are essential to prevent fatigue, which can affect a pilot's ability to perform their duties safely. Fatigue can impair cognitive function, decision-making, and reaction times, which can lead to errors and accidents.

The FAA also requires airlines to develop and implement a Fatigue Risk Management System (FRMS) to identify and mitigate the risk of fatigue in flight crews. The FRMS includes measures such as scheduling policies, training programs, and fatigue monitoring tools to ensure that flight crews are adequately rested.

In addition to the FAA regulations, the International Civil Aviation Organization (ICAO) has developed guidelines for rest time requirements for flight crews. These guidelines recommend that flight crews should have at least 10 hours of rest between duty periods, with a maximum of 14 hours of flight duty time per day.

In Europe pilots' rosters must adhere to all FTL Flight Time Limitations as stipulated in the EASA regulations which can be even more restrictive as adopted by the European Parliament of the European Commission proposal to harmonize flight and duty time limitations (FTL) for cabin crew and pilots across the European Union. Other regions in Latin America and Asia and all around the globe have regulations regarding rest time.

All airlines recognize the importance of rest time for flight crews and have implemented their own policies to ensure their flight crews are adequately rested.

As indicated in a study (Venus, M., & grosse Holtforth, M. 2022) *"...Chronic stress appears to be linked to psychophysiological wear and tear, and was associated with higher levels of fatigue, more sleep disturbances and more impaired mental health. Future research should not only consider fatigue as an immediate threat to aviation safety, but also as a significant threat to pilots' safety-relevant fitness to fly.."* [9]

Rest time requirements for flight crews are crucial to ensuring the safety of airline operations. The regulations and guidelines to ensure flight crews have enough rest periods to maintain their mental and physical health. As aviation professionals, it's essential to prioritize rest time and ensure that we are adequately rested before performing our duties. You must also take personal responsibility for your own sleep hygiene. This means making sure you are getting enough sleep, maintaining a regular sleep schedule, and avoiding activities that can disrupt your sleep, such as drinking caffeine or using electronic devices before bed.

Sleep is not just a matter of quantity, but also quality. Even if you are getting enough hours of sleep each night, if your sleep is frequently disrupted or of poor quality, you may still experience the effects of sleep deprivation. Try to create an environment that is conducive to quality sleep. This includes making sure your sleep environment is quiet, cool, and dark, and avoiding activities that can interfere with your sleep, such as working or watching TV in bed.

Recognize the role that mental health and well-being play in sleep hygiene. Anxiety, depression, and other mental health issues can all affect your ability to sleep, as can stress related to work or personal life. Take care of your mental health as well as your physical health. This may include seeking professional help if needed, practicing relaxation techniques such as meditation or deep breathing, or finding other ways to reduce stress in your life.

Sleep hygiene is a critical component of overall health and well-being, particularly. By prioritizing your sleep, you can help ensure that you are able to perform at your best and minimize the risk of errors or accidents related to fatigue.

Mitigating Jetlag

Mitigating the effects of jetlag and solving the age-old problem of disrupted sleep due to travel. I have spent many years working with aviation professionals and flight crews and the effects of sleep on the human body and how to optimize it is really a part of the lifestyle and profession. Here are some practical tips that can help you mitigate the effects of jetlag and sleep better while traveling and flying regularly.

Adjust your sleep schedule before your trip if you can.

If you are traveling across multiple time zones, it can be helpful to adjust your sleep schedule before you leave or at least to a degree that lessens the abrupt change of time. Adjusting your routine to the time change gradually can help your body get used to the new time zone that bit faster. Try to gradually shift your sleep schedule a few days before your trip to match the time zone of your destination. This may not always be possible for long haul pilots as just when you are about to get used to one destination you may be flying in the opposite direction to another time zone a few days later. In that case it would be an adapted version of this practice to optimize for best case scenario rather than expect to completely get rid of the challenging effects of jetlag.

Stay hydrated.

Dehydration can worsen the symptoms of jetlag, so it is essential to stay hydrated. Drink plenty of water before and during your flight, and while on the layover lower your intake of alcohol and caffeine, which can dehydrate you.

Get some sunlight.

Sunlight is a natural regulator of the body's circadian rhythm, which controls our sleep-wake cycle. Exposure to sunlight can help reset your body clock and adjust to the new time zone. Try to get outside and expose yourself to natural light as much as possible.

Take a nap.

A short nap can help you recharge and stay alert during the day. Keep it short, around 20-30 minutes, and avoid napping too close to bedtime, as this can interfere with your ability to fall asleep at night.

Avoid screens before bedtime.

The blue light emitted by electronic devices such as smartphones, tablets, and laptops can interfere with your body's natural production of melatonin, the hormone that regulates sleep. Try to avoid using these devices for at least an hour before bedtime to help you fall asleep faster.

Exercise

Try to move around and stretch during the flight. This will help improve blood flow and prevent muscle stiffness. Also, try to get some exercise once you arrive at your destination to help reset your body clock.

Always remember the regulations and policy regarding sleep aids

If you are still having trouble sleeping, you will have to review regulations and policy around using any sleep aids such as melatonin supplements or prescription medication as in the profession especially flight deck crews it may not be permitted for safety reasons. Ground personnel and other administrative areas of the industry may have different policy restrictions, but always consult your manuals and regulatory guidelines as well as company policy. It is essential to consult with your aeromedical doctor before considering taking any sleep aid, especially if you have any underlying health conditions or are taking other medications. Mitigating jetlag and improving sleep while traveling and flying regularly requires some planning and effort, but the benefits are well worth it. By following these practical tips, you can optimize your sleep and stay alert and refreshed during your travels. Of course, everyone's body is different, so it's important to listen to your body and do what works best for you. Remember, getting enough rest is essential for safe and effective performance in the aviation industry, so make sure to prioritize your sleep and take care of yourself both on and off the job.

Understand that wellbeing is not just about feeling happy or avoiding negative emotions. It is a holistic state that encompasses all aspects of our lives, including our physical health, mental clarity, and social connections.

There are also several practices that can help us achieve a state of complete wellbeing. These practices include:

Gratitude journaling. Writing down things we are grateful for each day can help us cultivate a positive mindset and increase feelings of happiness and fulfillment.

Engaging in hobbies and passions. Engaging in activities that bring us joy and fulfillment can help us increase feelings of happiness and overall wellbeing.

Achieving a state of complete wellbeing is a journey, not a destination. It takes time and effort to cultivate healthy habits and practices, but the rewards are immeasurable.

Here are a few suggestions on how you might begin to foster a sense of wellbeing in your own life. Perhaps you might try social connection through music. The power of music in bringing people together and fostering a sense of social connection is immense. We all know that special feeling when we go to a live event hosted by our favorite band or artist, it is pure magic. Go and enjoy live concerts and events and theatre on a regular basis. Explore creating a group playlist and sharing your favorite songs with each other as a way of building connections and creating positive emotions. You might look at creative expression through art and explore different forms of art as a way of expressing yourself. Experiment with different mediums such as painting, drawing, or sculpture, and discuss the benefits of using art as a form of self-expression. See if you like the experience and enjoy the activity.

Try mindful movement practices such as yoga or tai chi practices for physical and mental health. Incorporate a gratitude practice into their daily routine. You might start keeping a gratitude journal or sharing one thing they are grateful for each day.

Make more connection with nature. Visit local parks or nature reserves and try more outdoor pursuits out in nature such as trekking through forests or going hiking or cycling with friends. Join social walking clubs, and even though you may travel regularly, some of these clubs have affiliates in many cities around the world and are a great way to exercise and make social connections at the same time.

When you think of wellbeing, what comes to mind? Perhaps you think of exercise, a healthy diet, or meditation. While these are all important aspects of wellbeing, there is so much more to it than that. We need to understand that wellbeing is not a one-size-fits-all approach. What works for one person may not work for another. We are all unique individuals with unique needs and desires, and this must be taken into consideration when striving for wellbeing.

How can we achieve complete wellbeing? It starts with understanding the three key components, which I recap here physical, mental, and social.

Physical wellbeing includes taking care of our bodies through exercise, nutrition, and sleep. It also means avoiding harmful habits such as smoking and excessive alcohol consumption. But physical wellbeing also means something else, listening to our bodies. Too often we push ourselves too hard and ignore our physical needs. If we feel tired, we need to rest. If we feel pain, we need to seek medical attention. By listening to our bodies, we can prevent injury and maintain optimal physical health.

Mental wellbeing includes taking care of our emotional and psychological health. This includes managing stress and anxiety, seeking help when needed, and engaging in activities that bring us joy and fulfillment. Mental wellbeing also means being mindful of our thoughts and self-talk. Negative self-talk can be harmful and lead to feelings of depression and anxiety. By practicing positive self-talk, we can improve our mental wellbeing.

Social wellbeing includes building and maintaining positive relationships with others. This means connecting with others on a deeper level, being a good listener, and supporting one another. Social wellbeing also means setting healthy boundaries and knowing when to say no. By prioritizing healthy relationships, we can improve our overall wellbeing and sense of fulfillment. Meditation and mindfulness practices have proven to be very beneficial.

A study by (Murakami, H., et al, 2012) indicated that gray matter volume in certain parts of the brain such as the amygdala is significantly associated with a facet of the mindfulness tendency. The amygdala plays a primary role in psychological and physiological emotional responses.[10] The brains of meditators experienced physiological changes and effects in parts of the brain that can contribute to mental wellbeing in particular.

Coping Mechanisms

Coping is an essential aspect of emotional regulation and resilience, and it is vital for maintaining good mental health and wellbeing. Coping strategies are the actions and techniques we use to manage stress and emotional distress, and they can help us feel more in control and better equipped to deal with challenging situations.

There are many different types of coping strategies, and they can be broadly classified into two categories: problem-focused coping and emotion-focused coping. Problem-focused coping involves taking active steps to address the root cause of the stressor, such as seeking information, planning, or taking action to solve the problem. Emotion-focused coping, on the other hand, involves managing the emotional impact of the stressor, such as seeking social support, engaging in self-care activities, or using relaxation techniques.

Both types of coping can be effective in different situations, and it is essential to have a range of coping strategies available to us. However, some coping strategies are more effective than others, depending on the situation and the individual. For example, problem-focused coping may be more effective when dealing with a specific and controllable stressor, such as a work deadline, while emotion-focused coping may be more effective when dealing with a more significant and uncontrollable stressor, such as a natural disaster or accident or incident.

Not all coping strategies are healthy or helpful. Some coping strategies, such as substance use or avoidance, can be harmful and may exacerbate the problem in the long run. It is essential to be aware of our coping strategies and to choose those that are healthy, effective, and appropriate for the situation.

Here are some examples of healthy and effective coping strategies that can help enhance emotional wellbeing and resilience:

Exercise: Physical activity is an excellent way to reduce stress and boost mood. Exercise releases endorphins, which are natural mood-boosters, and can help reduce feelings of anxiety and depression.

Relaxation techniques. Mindfulness and relaxation techniques, such as deep breathing, meditation, and progressive muscle relaxation, can help reduce stress and promote relaxation.

Talking to friends, family, or a mental health professional can be an effective way to manage stress and cope with difficult emotions.

Cognitive restructuring. This involves changing the way we think about a stressor or problem and can help reduce negative emotions and increase feelings of control and optimism. We talked about this kind of reframing in detail in the section on it is what it is, and it's a part of life sections.

Engaging in activities that promote self-care, such as taking a bath, reading a book, or listening to music, can help reduce stress and promote emotional wellbeing.

By using a combination of these and other healthy coping strategies, individuals can enhance their emotional wellbeing and resilience, and better manage stress and difficult emotions. It all seems like common sense when laid out in simple terms here, but over the years I have come across many professionals who simply did not realize that the solutions can be so simple and effective. Instead, quite a few remained suffering in silence longer than necessary and some even burned out.

Coping with Incidents and Accidents

Coping with aviation accidents and trauma is a complex and challenging process, and it requires a range of psychological and emotional coping strategies. It is vital to engage with qualified experts with evidence-based approaches that are trained to assist industry professionals in these cases. An example of coping with aviation accidents and trauma is using peer support programs and CARE teams.

Peer support programs are designed to provide emotional and psychological support to those who have experienced traumatic events, such as aviation accidents. These programs involve trained peer supporters, who have themselves experienced similar traumas, and can provide a unique level of understanding and empathy to those who are struggling to cope.

After a fatal aviation accident, a peer support program could be established for the surviving family members and colleagues. The program would provide a safe space for participants to express their emotions, share their experiences, and receive emotional support and guidance from trained peers. This can help to promote feelings of connection, reduce isolation, and build resilience in the face of adversity.

In addition to peer support programs, other coping strategies include seeking professional help from trained mental health professionals, engaging in self-care activities such as exercise and relaxation techniques, and maintaining social connections with supportive friends and family members.

It is important to note that everyone copes with trauma and grief differently, and there is no one "right" way to cope. However, by engaging in a variety of coping strategies and seeking support when needed, individuals can build resilience and successfully navigate the challenging process of coping with aviation accidents and trauma.

Critical Incident Stress Management (CISM) teams are specialized groups of mental health professionals who are trained to respond to crises and provide support to individuals who have been affected by traumatic events, such as aviation accidents or other disasters. Some airlines set up Emergency Response Special Assistance Team (SAT), which can also be referred to as the CARE Team or Family Assistance Team, is the team that assists survivors and family members of injured survivors or fatalities in serious aircraft and aviation accidents and deploys a Go Team for set up of the Family Assistance Center. The purpose of these teams is to help individuals and communities to cope with the psychological impact of a crisis, reduce the risk of long-term mental health problems, and facilitate the process of recovery.

When responding to an aviation accident, a trained professional team may provide a range of services, including on-site support and debriefing for survivors, family members, and witnesses, as well as follow-up care and referrals to additional mental health services as needed. CARE team members may include mental health professionals, such as psychologists and social workers, as well as other trained volunteers, such as peer counselors, chaplains, and emergency response personnel.

CARE teams typically use a variety of techniques and interventions to help individuals and communities to cope with traumatic events. These may include:

Psychological first aid. This involves providing immediate support and assistance to individuals who have been affected by a crisis. Psychological first aid may include basic needs assessment, active listening, and practical support such as food, shelter, and transportation.

A critical incident stress debriefing is a structured group process that allows individuals to share their experiences, emotions, and reactions to a traumatic event in a supportive and safe environment. The goal of critical incident stress debriefing is to help individuals to process their feelings and experiences, reduce the risk of post-traumatic stress disorder (PTSD), and promote recovery.

Psychoeducation and coping strategies. CARE teams may provide information and education to individuals and communities about common reactions to trauma, coping strategies, and self-care techniques. This may include teaching relaxation techniques, providing resources for support groups or counseling services, and helping individuals to develop a personalized self-care plan.

Referrals and follow-up care, CARE teams may also provide referrals to additional mental health services as needed, such as counseling or medication. They may also follow up with individuals and communities to provide ongoing support and care.

In the context of COVID-19, CARE teams have been instrumental in providing support and resources to individuals and communities who have been affected by the pandemic. This may include providing virtual support groups, telehealth services, and online resources for coping with stress and anxiety related to the pandemic. More needs to be done however, and as another study indicates (Cullen, P., Gaynor, K. 2022) *"...feedback was obtained from over 3000 aviation workers. Survey feedback indicates that aviation workers are experiencing considerable challenges in relation to their health and wellbeing. These challenges are not being adequately addressed at an organisational level, which creates risk both from an individual and flight safety perspective..."*[11]

Observer and the other is the Experiencer.

When one is too feeling slightly overwhelmed within a set experience or sensation one can slide across the threshold into the Observer role, with its detachment, and do so by labelling, so that he what it feels like, that is anger, pleasure, pain or whatever. That dialogue in your head is between a detached observer and the experiencer is an ongoing thing.

The observer is the part of our mind that observes what is happening around us and within us. The experiencer is the part of our mind that experiences those observations. The two are separate but interconnected, and our inner dialogue is the conversation between them.

When we're in stressful situations, it's common for our inner dialogue to become chaotic and overwhelming. The observer may be taking in a lot of information, while the experiencer is feeling the stress of the situation. In this case, it's important to recognize the inner dialogue and take steps to calm it down.

An effective technique for calming the inner dialogue is to focus on the present moment. For example, if you're experiencing turbulence on a flight, focus on your breathing and the feeling of your feet on the ground. This helps to bring the observer and the experiencer back into alignment and reduces the impact of the inner dialogue.

The inner dialogue between the observer and the experiencer in our mind can have a significant impact on our performance. By being aware of this dialogue and taking steps to calm it down. This is where labelling and positive self-talk can really help. Phrases and mantras such as "I don't do panic" or "Easy does it, and you got this!" can help you steady that tight rope as you walk across it and try to settle your nerves. Your nervous system is translating the energy of your thoughts into your physiology and movement and behavior. Take a confident posture with your line of sight well above the horizon and maintain it for a period. Don't allow the tail to wag the dog and ensure that your physiology is consistent with your desired state.

Research has shown that imagining ourselves performing a task successfully can help improve our actual performance. If you're facing a high-pressure situation, take a few moments to visualize yourself handling it with calm competence. Imagine the details, the sights, the sounds, the sensations. And allow yourself to feel confident and capable. Pull yourself back from the edge and breathe deeply. Your breathing is essential in these cases.

I'd now like share with you the importance of breathing in maintaining control, calmness, and clear thinking in high-pressure situations.

Breathing is something we all do naturally without much thought, but did you know that the way we breathe can have a significant impact on our physical and mental states? When we are under stress, our breathing becomes shallow and quick, which can lead to increased heart rate, tension, and anxiety. However, by consciously regulating our breathing, we can activate the parasympathetic nervous system, which helps us relax and calm down.

An effective breathing technique to reduce stress and increase relaxation is called diaphragmatic breathing, also known as belly breathing. This technique involves breathing deeply into the belly, rather than shallowly into the chest. By taking slow, deep breaths, we can increase the flow of oxygen to our brain and muscles, which helps to reduce tension and clear our minds.

The other technique is called box breathing as we mentioned earlier, which involves inhaling for a count of four, holding the breath for a count of four, exhaling for a count of four, and then holding the breath for a count of four again before starting the cycle over. This technique can be particularly useful during moments of high stress or anxiety, as it helps to slow down our heart rate and reduce tension.

You see, when we breathe, we take in oxygen and release carbon dioxide. Oxygen is essential for our body's functions, including the production of energy. Did you know that breathing also plays a crucial role in regulating our nervous system?

When we breathe slowly and deeply, we activate our parasympathetic nervous system, which is responsible for calming our body and mind. This response reduces our heart rate, lowers our blood pressure, and promotes relaxation.

On the other hand, when we breathe quickly and shallowly, we activate our sympathetic nervous system, which is responsible for the fight-or-flight response. This response increases our heart rate, raises our blood pressure, and prepares our body to act. Understand how our breathing affects our nervous system and, in turn, our performance under pressure. By controlling our breath and activating our parasympathetic nervous system, we can maintain a clear mind, make better decisions, and perform at our best.

4-7-8 Breathing Exercise

To put it into practice, I suggest trying a simple breathing exercise called the 4-7-8 technique. Inhale through your nose for four seconds, hold your breath for seven seconds, then exhale through your mouth for eight seconds. Repeat this cycle several times, and you'll feel the calming effects in your body and mind. By understanding the science behind breath and practicing techniques like the 4-7-8 technique, we can maintain control, clarity, and calmness in even the most challenging situations. While combining this with posture and physiology control, as well as self-talk routines and mantras you will be armed with a useful toolkit for calming yourself down.

Breathing is a powerful tool that we can use to maintain control, calmness, and clear thinking in high-pressure situations. By consciously regulating our breath, we can activate the parasympathetic nervous system, reduce stress and tension, and improve our mental clarity.

Wellbeing through finding Meaning, Purpose and Fulfillment in your Personal and Professional Life.

I want to direct our attention to the importance of living a meaningful and fulfilling life and finding purpose in your work. One of the most important things to understand about finding meaning and fulfillment is that it is a deeply personal journey. What brings meaning and fulfillment to one person may not do the same for another. However, there are some common themes that I believe are essential to living a purposeful life and having a rewarding career.

The first is passion. Finding something that you are passionate about and pursuing it with dedication and perseverance can bring tremendous satisfaction and a sense of purpose to your life. This industry tends to draw folks that are passionate about it and that's what makes people stay in the field for their whole careers. Despite the many challenges and pressures, it's an exciting and inspiring business.

Some may be passionate about designing new aircraft or delivering the best customer service, and by dedicating themselves to that pursuit have found deep meaning and purpose in their work.

The second is curiosity. Maintaining a sense of curiosity and wonder about the world can lead to lifelong learning and growth, which can be deeply fulfilling. In the context of aviation and aerospace, this means staying up to date on the latest advancements in technology, learning about the history of flight, or exploring the magnificent possibilities of the future.

By staying curious in a childlike way continually asking questions and seeking answers, you will always have extraordinarily interesting things to discover and explore and perhaps design and invent. Always consider ways of improving processes, better ways to do things and ways of improving yourself.

The third is service. Finding ways to use your skills and knowledge to make a positive impact on the world can be incredibly fulfilling. This is a noble business, connecting people and goods all over the world. The magic of aviation and aerospace is inspiring. Reaching for the heavens and the stars. Never take for granted the great advances we have made, and how wonderful it is to be able to sit comfortably and travel around the world in magnificent machines we have designed and built and cruise above the clouds or marvel at how the space agencies are exploring our universe. Take pride that you are a part of that and be grateful for the opportunity every day to bring the best version of yourself to your family, friends, work colleagues and customers. Find meaning in service, find purpose in doing it better than ever before. To be top professional in all you do. Focus on attention to detail and delivering quality world class service. Thrive in your careers and always look at preparing the next generation of professionals coming after you. Through the constant ingenuity, creativity and skills of those that have come before us and countless professionals that have advanced the technology, processes, designs and invested and manufactured, take a moment to be grateful for all that. You can do that and more for the next generations to come through and or the benefit of humanity. Take pride in what you do, and constantly strive to do it as best you can.

Some will use their knowledge and experience to help educate and inspire others and that kind of service brings a sense of deep meaning and satisfaction to life. I feel blessed to be able to contribute in some way through this work to help others benefit from what I have learned over many years working in the industry. I am determined that the work be practical and easily applied. Similarly, you may find that using your expertise to make a positive impact on the world can be one of the most fulfilling aspects of your career. Enjoy your own personal journey in pursuit of excellence and wellbeing that requires dedication, curiosity, and a commitment to service. By pursuing your passions, maintaining a sense of curiosity and wonder, and finding ways to make a positive impact on the world, you can find deep meaning and purpose in your work and your life. Building connections and relationships with others can bring a great sense of fulfillment and meaning to our lives and is a large contributor to our own wellbeing. The satisfaction of collaborating with colleagues on a project or mission or working with members of the community to promote the benefits of aviation and space travel is very rewarding. I have always found that connecting with others and sharing ideas and knowledge was one of the most rewarding aspects of my work as an aviation professional. By building relationships with other professionals, personnel and instructors, I was able to expand my own understanding of the industry and develop new ideas and insights. It is also important to find time for other activities and relationships that bring joy and meaning to our lives. Whether it is spending time with loved ones, pursuing hobbies, or engaging in community service, finding a balance between work and other aspects of life can help us maintain a sense of fulfillment and happiness in the long run. Make sure that you pay attention to work life balance.

Ikigai "a reason for being."

I would like to touch briefly upon a concept called ikigai, which has its roots in Japanese culture and has been found to have significant benefits for personal fulfillment and success. Ikigai is a simple yet powerful concept that helps us understand our purpose in life. It translates to "a reason for being" and is the intersection of four things: what you love, what you are good at, what the world needs, and what you can be paid for. Finding your ikigai can lead to a sense of direction and fulfillment, both in your personal and professional life.

Here we will consider the four components of ikigai.

The first is what you love. This refers to your passion, the things that make you happy and that you enjoy doing. For aviation and aerospace professionals, this might be the thrill of flying or the excitement of working on cutting-edge technology.

The second is what you are good at. This refers to your skills and talents. It's important to recognize your strengths and work to develop them further. As aviation and aerospace professionals, this might be your technical knowledge or your ability to work well and for ground personnel it could be talent for solving problems and getting aircraft turned around on time, for an aircraft mechanic it could be a talent for diagnosing and fixing problems efficiently and for pilots it could be great airmanship.

The third is what the world needs. This refers to what the world needs and how you can make a positive impact. This might be creating safer and more efficient ways to travel or developing technology that can help solve global challenges.

The fourth is what you can be paid for. This refers to the practical aspect of finding your purpose. It's important to find a career that can support you financially while also aligning with your passions, skills, and impact.

When you find your ikigai, you will experience a sense of flow and purpose that can lead to greater success and happiness. It's not always easy to find your ikigai, but there are some steps you can take to get closer to it. Start by exploring your passions and interests, identifying your strengths and weaknesses, and thinking about how you can make a positive impact in the world.

SECTION 3

PERFORMANCE OPTIMIZATION FOR PROFESSIONAL EXCELLENCE

The Brain

The brain is not a static organ - it changes and adapts throughout our lives. This process is known as neuroplasticity, and it's the brain's ability to reorganize itself by forming new neural connections.

We use this knowledge to enhance performance through the concept of "brain training" and simulations. Just like we train our bodies through exercise, we can train our brains to become more efficient and effective and the practice in full flight simulators achieves exactly the kind of changes in the brain that occur when one is flying an aircraft. Practice and training in the simulators are so realist that it is considered practically the same as if it had been performed on an actual aircraft.

There are several other ways to engage in brain training, including cognitive training exercises, mindfulness practices, and even physical exercise. Cognitive training exercises can involve tasks such as memory games, problem-solving puzzles, and attentional exercises. These types of exercises have been shown to enhance cognitive performance and improve overall brain health. The key is novelty, it should be a new task, and not just repeatedly doing the same puzzles such as sudoku or the likes.

Meditation has also been shown to have a positive impact on brain function.

Physical exercise is not only beneficial for our physical health, but also for our brain health. Exercise has been shown to increase neuroplasticity, improve memory, and even enhance cognitive flexibility.

In the aviation and aerospace industries, these brain training techniques can be applied in several ways. Pilots and astronauts can engage in cognitive training exercises to enhance their attention, memory, and decision-making abilities. Mindfulness practices can be used to reduce stress and improve focus during high-pressure situations.

And physical exercise can be used to enhance overall brain health and cognitive performance.

Brain Performance and Enhancement.

Our brain is one of the most complex organs in our body, and it's responsible for everything we think, feel, and do. Just like other muscles in our body, it can be trained and enhanced through the right kind of practices and activities.

Physical exercise increases the blood flow to the brain, which helps to nourish and maintain healthy brain cells. Aerobic exercise is particularly beneficial, as it helps to increase the production of growth factors that support the growth and survival of new neurons in the brain. Our brains thrive on new experiences and challenges, and it's essential to provide it with the right kind of mental stimulation to keep it active and healthy. Engaging in activities that require problem-solving, critical thinking, and creativity can help to enhance our brain's performance and increase our cognitive abilities.

Our brain needs adequate rest and sleep to function at its best. Sleep is essential for memory consolidation, learning, and overall brain health. Getting enough sleep can help to improve our cognitive abilities, including our attention span, memory, and problem-solving skills. Nutrition is also a critical factor in brain performance and enhancement. Our brain needs the right kind of nutrients to function at its best. A diet rich in omega-3 fatty acids, antioxidants, and other brain-boosting nutrients can help to improve our cognitive abilities and overall brain health. All these health and performance enhancing insights will help you to not only improve your medical exam results but also contribute to your wellbeing and quality of life.

Did you know that some astronauts have reported experiencing a phenomenon called the "overview effect" while in space? This is a cognitive shift in awareness that occurs when seeing the Earth from the perspective of outer space. Astronauts have described feeling a sense of unity with humanity and a heightened awareness of the fragility of our planet.

This experience can be linked to the Power of Mental Force because it highlights the incredible ability of the human brain to perceive the world in new and transformative ways. By challenging our preconceptions and opening ourselves up to new experiences, we can unlock more of the potential of our minds.

Aviators can take several steps to avoid brain fog, including:

- Getting enough sleep. Lack of sleep can lead to cognitive impairment, memory problems, and difficulty focusing, which can contribute to brain fog. Aviators should prioritize getting adequate sleep and establishing a regular sleep schedule to avoid sleep deprivation.
- Staying hydrated. Dehydration can also contribute to brain fog, as it can affect cognitive function and impair concentration. Aviators should make sure to drink enough water and other fluids throughout the day, especially during long flights.
- Eating a balanced diet. Proper nutrition is essential for brain function, and a diet that is high in processed or sugary foods can lead to brain fog. Aviators should aim to eat a balanced diet that includes whole grains, fruits and vegetables, lean protein, and healthy fats.
- Taking breaks. Extended periods of concentration or mental exertion can lead to fatigue and brain fog. Aviators should take regular breaks during flights, especially on long flights, to give their brains a chance to rest and recharge.
- Practicing stress management techniques. Stress can also contribute to brain fog, so aviators should practice stress management techniques such as meditation, deep breathing exercises, or yoga to help reduce stress levels.

By taking these steps, aviators can help reduce their risk of experiencing brain fog and maintain their cognitive function and focus during flights.

Aviators can take several steps to avoid confusion and maintain clear thinking when disoriented or overwhelmed by stimuli or workload. Please bear in mind that these are ideas, however crew members should follow all regulatory and company policies and standard operating procedures in relation to these issues. Here are some tips as to possible approaches,

- Communicate with your crew. Seeking assistance from the captain or co-pilot is vital when an aviator is experiencing confusion or cognitive overload. The captain and co-pilot are trained to work as a team and can help each other manage workload and maintain situational awareness. In fact, it is common practice for pilots to communicate with each other and cross-check each other's actions and decisions to ensure that they are both on the same page and that the flight is proceeding safely. During multiple alarms or malfunctions and a lot of confusing information, the crew member may refer to the other crew member for clarification example "Have you any better ideas?" "Do you have any suggestions on how to solve this issue?"

In such situations where an aviator is experiencing cognitive overload, it can be helpful to ask for assistance from the other pilot, who may be better able to maintain situational awareness and help manage the workload. This can also help to prevent errors or accidents that could result from the aviator's reduced ability to process information and make decisions.

- It is important for aviators to maintain open communication with their fellow crew members and to work together as a team to ensure that the flight proceeds safely and efficiently.

- Prioritize and focus on the most critical tasks. When under pressure, it's easy to get overwhelmed by the sheer volume of tasks and information. By prioritizing and focusing on the most critical tasks, aviators can stay on track and avoid getting bogged down in unimportant details. We will discuss the priority list of aviate, navigate and communicate in just a moment.
- Use checklists. Checklists are an essential tool for ensuring that nothing is overlooked, and all necessary steps are taken. They can help aviators stay organized and reduce the cognitive load associated with complex tasks.
- Regularly practice stress management techniques. High levels of stress can impair cognitive function and lead to confusion and poor decision-making. Aviators can reduce stress by practicing relaxation techniques such as deep breathing, meditation, or yoga.
- Practice situational awareness. Situational awareness involves being aware of one's surroundings and the context in which tasks are being performed. This can help aviators anticipate potential problems and respond proactively.
- Use visual aids and quick reference guides. Visual aids such as quick reference guides, maps, diagrams, manuals and charts can help aviators process information more efficiently and reduce cognitive overload.
- Take short breaks when possible. Taking short breaks can help aviators recharge and maintain focus. Even a brief rest can help alleviate stress and improve cognitive function.

Communication is key in these situations and it's important for your team to know if you are unclear about anything. You should be very clear about instructions and what you need to do, and when unsure follow your standard operating procedures and regulations in those instances.

Optimum spatial awareness is critical for aviators to safely navigate through the airspace. Here are some key factors that can help enhance spatial awareness:

Visual scanning. Aviators should develop the habit of scanning their environment and checking their instruments frequently to maintain situational awareness. They should use the "Scan and Interpret" method, which involves scanning the horizon for reference points, interpreting their position relative to those points, and adjusting accordingly.

Mental mapping. Pilots should develop a mental map of their surroundings and the airspace in which they are flying. This involves creating a mental picture of the terrain, landmarks, airports, and airspace structures in their area.

Instrument proficiency. Aviators should be proficient in using their aircraft's instruments and navigation systems to enhance their spatial awareness. They should be able to quickly and accurately interpret their instruments and use that information to make informed decisions.

Training. Regular training and practice can help aviators improve their spatial awareness skills. This can include simulators, flight training, and ground school instruction.

Attention to detail. Aviators should pay close attention to details in their environment, such as changes in the weather, terrain, or other aircraft. They should also be aware of their own physical and mental state, such as fatigue or stress, which can impact their spatial awareness.

Teamwork. In multi-crew aircraft, effective communication and teamwork can help enhance spatial awareness. Pilots should work together to cross-check each other's instruments and maintain situational awareness.

Optimum spatial awareness requires a combination of visual scanning, mental mapping, instrument proficiency, training, attention to detail, and teamwork. By developing these skills and habits, aviators can enhance their situational awareness and safely navigate through the airspace.

Brain Hemisphere Synchronization

Brain hemisphere synchronization can lead to improved cognitive abilities such as increased creativity, problem-solving skills, and overall mental clarity. This is because when the two hemispheres of the brain are working together in harmony, they can access and process information more efficiently.

One way to achieve brain hemisphere synchronization is through activities that require the use of both hemispheres, such as playing musical instruments, engaging in physical exercise, or practicing meditation. Additionally, certain types of music, such as binaural beats, have been shown to promote brain synchronization when listened to with headphones. By training the brain to work in harmony, pilots and other aviation professionals can better manage stress and make more effective decisions in complex and uncertain operational scenarios. By training the brain to function more cohesively and efficiently, pilots can increase the odds to enhance their situational awareness and response time in emergency situations. For creative teams such as the aerospace and aircraft design engineers Another potential benefit of brain hemisphere synchronization is increased creativity and innovation. By tapping into both the logical and intuitive aspects of the brain, individuals may be able to approach problems in new and unique ways, leading to breakthroughs and advancements in the aviation and aerospace industries. Achieving brain hemisphere synchronization is easier said than done. It requires consistent practice and dedication. The potential benefits are worth the effort for anyone looking to enhance their mental performance and well-being.

Heart and Brain Coherence

The human heart has a complex and sophisticated electromagnetic field, which can influence our overall health and well-being. The rhythmic beating of the heart produces an electromagnetic field that can be measured several feet away from the body. The study by *O Burlesen, K., Schwartz, G., 2004) states "..First, the heart as it contracts in systole, also rotates and produces torsion due to the structure of the myocardium. Second, the heart produces a significant electromagnetic field with each contraction due to the coordinated depolarization of myocytes producing a current flow.."[12] This field can interact with the fields of other living beings, including other people.

I would suggest that the heart has a significant impact on our mental and emotional states. For example, when we experience positive emotions like love, gratitude, and compassion, the heart's electromagnetic field becomes more coherent and harmonious. This coherence is associated with a state of improved mental clarity, emotional stability, and overall physical well-being. Conversely, negative emotions like anger, fear, and anxiety can cause the heart's electromagnetic field to become disordered and chaotic. This incoherence can lead to a state of mental and emotional turbulence, which can negatively impact our health. By increasing cardiac coherence, we can improve energy efficiency and bioinformation from the cardio electromagnetic field, which can lead to improved cardiovascular health.

Some therapies that can help improve cardiac coherence and overall well-being include heart rate variability training, mindfulness meditation, and other stress-reduction techniques. By cultivating positive emotions and reducing stress, we can improve our overall health and well-being and promote a more holistic approach to healing.

Understanding the energy of the heart and its impulses, and how they can be used to create coherence and harmony, can have profound implications for our physical, mental, and emotional health. By taking a holistic approach to healing and incorporating therapies that promote cardiac coherence, we can achieve improved overall well-being and a more fulfilling life.

Brain Wave Coherence and Heart Coherence.

Our brains and hearts are constantly emitting energy forms and wave patterns, which can sometimes be erratic and out of sync. We can synchronize the energy forms and wave patterns of our brain and heart, it can bring about a state of coherence and harmony, which has a positive impact on our physical, mental, and emotional wellbeing. Brain wave coherence refers to the synchronization of electrical activity in the brain, specifically the alpha and beta brain waves. When our brain waves are in sync, we are better able to focus, learn, and retain information. Heart coherence, on the other hand, refers to the synchronization of the *rhythmic pattern of the heart's energy pulses*, specifically the heart rate variability. When our heart rate variability is in sync, it has been shown to reduce stress and anxiety.

To achieve both brain wave coherence and heart coherence, there are several techniques that have been shown to be effective. One such technique is meditation, which has been shown to increase both brain wave coherence and heart coherence. Another technique is deep breathing exercises, which can help to slow down the heart rate and bring about a state of relaxation. Physical exercise and spending time in nature have also been shown to increase coherence in both the brain and heart.

As we continue to learn more about the energy forms and wave patterns of our brain and heart, it is becoming increasingly clear that by synchronizing them, we can achieve a state of coherence and harmony that can lead to greater physical, mental, and emotional wellbeing. It is an exciting area of research that has the potential to lead to new therapies for a range of conditions, including cardiovascular disease, anxiety, and depression.

To practice harmonizing brain wave coherence and heart energy pulse synchronization, I suggest starting with a deep breathing exercise. Begin by sitting comfortably and taking several deep breaths, allowing your body to relax and your mind to clear. Count backwards from 10 to 1 focusing on your breath as you do.

Now, focus your attention on your heart center, the area in the center of your chest. Imagine a warm, glowing light in this area, expanding with each breath you take. As you breathe in, visualize this light growing brighter and more intense, and as you breathe out, imagine it radiating outwards, enveloping your entire body.

As you continue to focus on your heart center and breathing deeply, begin to bring your attention to your brain waves. Imagine the electrical activity in your brain becoming synchronized and harmonized, with all parts of your brain working together in coherence. You can further enhance this practice by incorporating affirmations or visualization techniques in a variant such as follows.

Exercise

First, find a comfortable seated position with your spine straight and shoulders relaxed. Close your eyes and take a few deep breaths to relax your body and mind.

Next, focus your attention on your heart center and feel its rhythmic energy pulses. Allow your awareness to expand to your brain and notice the sensations in your head as you relax deeper and deeper. As you inhale, imagine breathing in pure, positive energy into your heart and brain. With each exhale, imagine releasing any negative thoughts or emotions. Now, visualize a beam of light connecting your heart and brain. Inhale and imagine this beam of light getting brighter and stronger. As you exhale, imagine any obstacles or resistance to this connection melting away. As you continue to focus on the heart-brain connection, repeat the following affirmations to yourself:

"My heart and brain are in perfect harmony."

"I am calm, focused, and in control."

"I radiate positive energy and attract abundance into my life."

Repeat these affirmations for several minutes, allowing yourself to sink deeper into a state of relaxation and coherence.

When you're ready to finish the exercise, take a deep breath in and exhale fully. Open your eyes and take a moment to notice how you feel - perhaps more centered, calm, and connected.

This exercise combines the principles of brain wave coherence and heart coherence to create a simple practice for harmonizing the mind and body.

Higher Purpose and Transcendence

The journey towards higher purpose and transcendence is a deeply personal and spiritual one, and it can be challenging and transformative. It involves a willingness to look beyond ourselves and our immediate concerns and connect with something greater, whether that be a divine force, nature, or the universe.

To embark on this journey, it's important to first take time to reflect on our values and beliefs, and to clarify what we feel is our purpose in life. This can involve exploring our passions and interests, examining our past experiences and how they have shaped us, and considering what we feel is our unique contribution to the world.

From there, we can begin to cultivate practices that help us connect with our higher selves and with the universe. This can involve meditation, prayer, mindfulness, or other spiritual practices that resonate with us. These practices can help us quiet the mind, connect with our inner wisdom, and tap into a sense of peace and harmony.

As a pilot, the concept of higher purpose and transcendence can be particularly meaningful. Every time we take off into the sky, we are essentially transcending the limitations of gravity and entering a new realm of experience. We are connected to the earth and yet separate from it, with a unique perspective on the world below us.

This sense of transcendence can be a powerful reminder of the bigger picture and our place in it. By realizing it is an honorable profession and focusing on the larger purpose of our work, whether it is to transport passengers safely or deliver important cargo or fly rockets to the moon and beyond we can tap into a deeper sense of meaning and fulfillment.

Moreover, this sense of higher purpose can extend beyond just the practical aspects of flying. As pilots, pilots and aviators and astronauts you have a responsibility to uphold the highest standards of professionalism, safety, and integrity. You are representing not only yourselves but also the aviation industry. By keeping this higher purpose in mind, you can approach our work with a sense of reverence and dedication. The air forces are particularly good at fostering this sense of greater good and passion for serving. To cultivate a greater sense of transcendence and higher purpose, there are a few practices that can be helpful. One is to take time before each flight, duty or mission to reflect on the purpose of your work and what you hope to accomplish. This can be done through meditation, journaling, or simply quiet contemplation. Another practice is to stay connected to the larger aviation community and the impact that flying has on the world. This might involve attending industry events or staying informed on the latest developments in aviation and aerospace technology and safety.

Ultimately, the journey towards higher purpose and transcendence is a deeply personal one. It requires an ongoing commitment to self-reflection, growth, and a willingness to look beyond the practicalities of flying to the deeper meaning and impact of our work.

Connecting with our Higher Self

The concept of higher and inner self refers to a deeper level of consciousness that exists within each of us. It is the part of us that is beyond our thoughts, beliefs, and experiences, and is often described as our true essence or soul. The higher self is the part of us that is connected to the universe and all living beings, while the inner self is the part of us that is more personal and individual.

By accessing a deeper inner level of consciousness, you may tap into a source of inner strength and wisdom that can help you navigate through difficult situations with greater ease and confidence.

A way to connect with the higher and inner self is through self-reflection and self-discovery. By exploring their values, beliefs, and life purpose, pilots can gain a deeper understanding of themselves and their place in the world. This can help you align your actions and decisions with their true essence, leading to greater fulfillment and success both personally and professionally.

Ultimately, connecting with the higher and inner self is about accessing a deeper level of consciousness and tapping into our true essence. This can be a powerful tool for navigating the challenges of work and finding greater fulfillment and meaning in their lives. Your inner self is the real you, and the source of your strength and wisdom, you tune into it by giving attention to that level of mind and allow it to work through you, and you may also refer to the section on getting out of your own way regarding how to tap into this level of being. We all have a choice to either continue living our lives on autopilot, following the norms and expectations of society, or to awaken to our inner self and discover our true purpose in life. The inner self can guide us towards our own individual destiny. Dwell upon the interconnectedness of all living things, and your ability to tap into a higher power beyond oneself. It involves tapping into our own inner power and connecting with a higher, more expansive perspective.

Commit to the practice of self-awareness, reflection, and growth in order to connect with our inner selves and realize our own potential. That way, we can access the wisdom and guidance that lies within us and use it to create a more fulfilling and purposeful life.

The journey towards higher purpose and transcendence is not an easy one, and requires us to confront our own fears, doubts, and limitations. We have the power within us to rise above these challenges and become the best versions of ourselves. Over time and through life experience we encounter different aspects of ourselves and challenges that we must overcome. We must learn to access our inner resources, including wisdom, compassion, courage, and strength, to navigate through life's ups and downs. Our inner self is already free and enlightened, but we need to remove the ignorance and delusion that keeps us from realizing this truth. To gain a better realization of our own being.

"Aviate, Navigate, Communicate."

"Aviate, navigate, communicate" is a commonly used phrase in aviation that represents the three main priorities that pilots should follow in order to ensure the safety of their flight.

- The priority, "aviate," means that the pilot's primary focus should be on controlling the aircraft and maintaining its stability and safety. This includes monitoring airspeed, altitude, and other critical flight parameters.
- The second priority, "navigate," means that the pilot should be aware of the aircraft's position and ensure that it is on course to reach its destination safely. This includes navigating using instruments, following flight plans, and maintaining situational awareness of the surrounding airspace.
- The third priority, "communicate," means that the pilot should maintain communication with air traffic control and other relevant parties to ensure that they are aware of the aircraft's position, intentions, and any issues that may arise during the flight.

Following these priorities in order to help pilots ensure the safety of their flight and prevent distractions or other issues from taking priority over critical flight tasks.

Mantras as an Aid to Alter your State.

I recall watching a documentary about Steve Mc Queen and the director explained how he used the device of a mantra and gave it to Steve to repeat throughout filming of a movie. The purpose of the mantra was as an aid or device to get McQueen into the right frame of mind and develop a persona around it. Apparently, it was effective in getting him into the right frame of mind and that came across in his screen presence. It occurred to me that this mental tool would be a useful addition to our mental tool kit. The use of mantras can in my opinion be a useful tool for individuals in many fields, including aviation. Mantras are short, positive statements that are repeated frequently to help focus the mind and create a positive mindset or a characteristic change in state or persona.

In the context of aviation, a mantra can be used to help pilots get into the right mindset for flying. This can help them to feel more confident, focused, poised and in control. It may be a short phrase that represents the qualities or characteristics that the pilot wants to embody while flying. For example, a pilot might choose a mantra like "I am calm, focused, and in control" or "I trust my training and experience." This phrase can be repeated silently to oneself prior to the flight.

Using a mantra can also help pilots to create a clear mental image of themselves as capable and confident aviators. This can be particularly helpful in situations where they might feel uncertain or overwhelmed. By repeating a mantra that reinforces positive beliefs about themselves and their abilities, pilots can stay focused and in control, even in challenging situations. This of course is an application of autosuggestion. Cabin crew can also use them to create a mental field of immunity to difficult and demanding customers and or colleagues. It can act as a mental shield if properly employed.

Motive and Opportunity

We can influence our behaviors by studying the ways human behavior works in other fields and apply the lessons to our own discipline. Motive and desire are powerful psychological forces that can greatly influence our behavior. Motive refers to the reason why someone may be driven to do something, while desire refers to a strong feeling of wanting or wishing for something. Motive can be divided into two categories: intrinsic and extrinsic. Intrinsic motives come from within a person and are driven by internal desires such as personal growth, curiosity, and self-expression. Extrinsic motives, on the other hand, come from external sources such as rewards, recognition, and praise. Desire, on the other hand, is often driven by emotional needs such as the desire for love, acceptance, power, or security. Desires can be positive, for example to help others or make a positive impact in the world, or negative, in the case of the desire for revenge or to harm others. Both motive and desire are powerful drivers of behavior, and they often work in tandem to influence our decisions and actions. For example, a person may be motivated to achieve a certain goal because it aligns with their intrinsic values and desires, or they may be motivated by the external rewards and recognition that come with achieving the goal.

Understanding our own motives and desires, as well as those of others, can be a key factor in promoting positive behavior. By aligning our actions with our intrinsic motives and desires, we can achieve a sense of purpose and fulfillment, and by recognizing and addressing the underlying emotional needs that drive negative desires, we can work to mitigate harmful behavior.

Opportunity, Proximity and Availability

The opportunities presented by proximity and availability are vast, but they also come with a certain level of responsibility. When we are near someone or something, we are more likely to engage with them, whether consciously or unconsciously. This can be a powerful tool when we want to influence positive behavior in ourselves or others. You can begin to engineer and design things so that you are close to the desired conditions, environments and people you want to engage with.

For example, if we want to encourage someone to exercise more, we can make sure that they have access to a gym or a nearby park where they can walk or run. By providing them with the opportunity and proximity to exercise, we increase the likelihood that they will engage in physical activity. This is about increasing the odds in your favor to have a probability of an outcome closer to what you desire.

On the other hand, this principle can also be used to encourage negative behaviors. For example, if we live in an area with a high concentration of fast-food restaurants, we are more likely to consume unhealthy food because of its availability and proximity. This is why it's important to be aware of our environment and the opportunities it presents. Use proximity and availability to increase the likelihood of positive behavior when used responsibly and strategically. We must be aware of our environment and the opportunities it presents and make conscious decisions about how we want to engage with those opportunities. Design things in such a way that it is more convenient and accessible to do the right behavior rather than an undesirable behavior. Active avoidance of scenarios that associate and trigger negative behaviors is an important way to help regain control of your circumstances.

If you want to learn more about flying go to the local flying club, engage with the people and instructors there, if you want to know more about air and space join the societies and organizations that have a common interest.

Drivers of Behavior

Psychological forces play a critical role in driving behavior. These forces can include factors such as past experiences, personal values, beliefs, and emotions. Our past experiences shape our perception of the world and affect our behavior, as we tend to behave in ways that we have learned to be effective in the past. This is why past traumas or damage continue to play such a pivotal role in the behavior of so many. Our personal values and beliefs also guide our actions, as they provide us with a framework for making decisions and determining what is important to us. Emotions can be particularly powerful drivers of behavior, as they are often tied to our most basic instincts and can override our rational decision-making processes. When it comes to behavior, psychological forces can be both positive and negative. Positive psychological forces, such as a strong sense of purpose or a commitment to personal values, can motivate us to act in ways that are consistent with our goals and values. Negative psychological forces, such as fear, anger, or anxiety, can also drive our behavior, but often in ways that are counterproductive or harmful.

Recognize the role that psychological forces play in driving our behavior, as this can help us to better understand why we behave the way we do. When we gain insight into the psychological forces that drive our behavior, we can work to change or redirect those forces in more positive ways. This can include learning to manage our emotions more effectively, challenging our beliefs and values to ensure that they are aligned with our goals, and using psychological techniques to become more aware of our thought patterns and habits.

Lessons on Peak performance from Formula 1.

As an aviation and aerospace professional there are several parallels between what you do and what other elite performers do in their respective fields. Some of the lessons and skills that are required in one field of discipline can be useful for other fields. For example, the precision required in Formula 1 driving and the skills they attain could be effectively applied by high performance pilots.

Formula 1 driving is a high-performance sport that requires a combination of physical and mental skills to be the best. It's not just about being fast but being precise and consistent. Here are some tips learned from Formula 1 that can help you develop the skills to be the best and perform at an elite level:

Practice Makes Perfect. The more time you spend behind the wheel, the better you will become. The same applies to the cockpit in fighter jets for example. Repetition is key to developing muscle memory and improving your reaction time. You need to put in the time and effort to master your craft.

Mental Preparation. Formula 1 driving is as mental as it is physical. You need to be mentally sharp and focused at all times. Meditation, visualization, and breathing exercises are just a few techniques that can help you develop mental focus and control.

Know Your Car. To be successful in Formula 1 driving, you need to understand your car and how it responds to different driving conditions. Spend time with your team and learn everything you can about your car's capabilities and limitations. In the case of pilots know your aircraft well and know your planes' capabilities and limitations.

Analyze Your Performance. Analyzing your performance after each race or practice session is crucial to identifying areas where you can improve. You need to be honest with yourself and willing to make changes to improve your performance. This is an important element in cybernetic type learning, in that you evaluate and learn from all performances.

Physical Fitness. Formula 1 driving is physically demanding, and you need to be in top physical condition to perform at an elite level. A healthy diet, regular exercise, and adequate rest are essential to maintaining peak physical performance.

Surround Yourself with a Great Team. You can't do it alone. Surround yourself with a team of professionals who can support you in your quest for success. This includes your team manager, engineers, mechanics, and other support staff. Same applies to aviation.

Success in Formula 1 driving, as in any endeavor, requires perseverance. You will face challenges and setbacks, but you need to stay focused on your goal and keep pushing forward.

Just as becoming a pilot or astronaut, becoming an elite Formula 1 driver requires dedication, hard work, and a willingness to learn and grow. By following studying and applying these lessons and putting in the time and effort, you can develop the skills to be the best and perform at an elite level.

Use Unconventional Training Methods to Enhance your Skills.

It can also mean taking unconventional approaches to enhance performance. For example, I was interested to hear a Formular 1 champion driver mention that he felt surfing was a great training aid for him. Here's why I believe he may have a point. Now, you may be wondering how surfing can be useful for aviation professionals. Well, let me explain. Surfing is a great way to train your balance, coordination, and reflexes. It requires you to constantly adjust your body position and movements to stay on the board and ride the waves. This is not so different from what you need to do as a pilot. As a pilot, you need to have excellent balance and coordination to handle the controls of your aircraft. You need to be able to react quickly and accurately to changing conditions and unexpected events. Surfing can help you develop these skills by challenging you to adapt to a constantly changing and unpredictable environment. It can teach you how to stay focused and alert in rapidly changing environments.

If you're looking for an unconventional way to train and improve your skills as an aviation professional, I highly why not give surfing a try. Even if you're not a great surfer, you can still benefit from the experience and have a lot of fun in the process.

Martial arts too can be a great unconventional training aid in several ways. Just like surfing, martial arts require a great deal of balance, focus, and coordination, which can be improved through regular training. Martial arts require practitioners to be present in the moment and react quickly to changes in their environment. Through the practice of martial arts, individuals can learn to remain calm and focused in high-pressure situations, as well as develop quick reflexes and the ability to think on their feet. It also teaches important values such as discipline, respect, and perseverance, which are essential not only for success in the martial arts, but also in other areas of life, including aviation.

Habits

Habits are the building blocks of our lives, and if we can design them to work for us instead of against us, we can achieve incredible success. A habit is a behavior that has been repeated enough times to become automatic. We all have habits, both good and bad, that we perform every day without even thinking about them. But the good news is that we can change our habits by understanding how they work and using that knowledge to our advantage. One of the key principles to designing successful habits is to make them small and specific. Instead of trying to change everything at once, focus on one small habit that will move you towards your goal. For example, if your goal is to improve your physical fitness, start by doing five push-ups every morning. It may seem small, but over time, those five push-ups will lead to more and more until you've built a habit of daily exercise.

Another principle is to make your habits visible. If you can see your habits, you're more likely to stick to them. For example, if you want to drink more water throughout the day, place a water bottle on your desk where you can see it. Seeing the bottle will remind you to drink more water and make it easier to create the habit.

Create a supportive environment for your habits. Surround yourself with people who support your goals and avoid those who might hinder your progress. For example, if your goal is to reduce your caffeine intake, try to avoid spending time in coffee shops or with friends who drink a lot of coffee.

Track your progress. Keep a record of your habits and the progress you've made. This will help you stay motivated and provide a sense of accomplishment as you see how far you've come.

Let's say you start a new habit of exercising every morning before work. First, you need to identify a cue or trigger for this habit. In this case, it might simply be putting on workout clothes as soon as you wake up or leaving them ready beside the bed. This will act as a signal to your brain that it's time to exercise.

Next, you need to create a small, manageable action that follows this cue. It could be something as simple as doing 5 push-ups or going for a 10-minute walk. The key is to make the action so easy that it's hard to say no.

Once you've completed the action, reward yourself with something that reinforces the habit. This could be as simple as a few minutes of relaxation or listening to your favorite music. By consistently following this process of cue-action-reward, you'll begin to form a new habit that will eventually become automatic. Once you've formed a habit, it becomes much easier to stick to your goals and make progress towards achieving them.

Emotional Intelligence

Psychologists Peter Salovey and John D. Mayer first introduced the concept of emotional intelligence back in 1990. Emotional intelligence refers to the ability to perceive, understand, and regulate emotions in oneself and others. It is composed of four dimensions: self-awareness, self-regulation, social awareness, and relationship management.

Emotional intelligence is essential for effective communication, decision-making, and teamwork. Pilots and crew members for example, must be able to work together cohesively, manage stress effectively, and make quick decisions in intense workload situations. I recommend training programs incorporate elements of the four dimensions of emotional intelligence. Training programs can teach individuals to recognize and understand their own emotions and the emotions of others, manage their emotions in stressful situations, and communicate effectively with others.

Organizations can promote a culture that supports emotional intelligence by fostering open communication, encouraging feedback, and creating a sense of teamwork and collaboration. This culture can help to create a positive work environment, enhance safety, and improve performance.

Salovey and Mayer's work on emotional intelligence has made significant contributions to our understanding of how to develop and apply emotional intelligence in various fields, including aviation and aerospace. By focusing on emotional intelligence, the aviation and aerospace industry can create a more effective and efficient workforce while also promoting safety and reducing errors.

Here are some ways in which emotional intelligence can be leveraged to achieve these goals.

Communication is a vital component of the aviation and aerospace industry, and effective communication is essential for safety and efficiency. By developing emotional intelligence, pilots and crew members can better understand their own emotions and the emotions of others, allowing them to communicate more effectively and resolve conflicts more efficiently. This can help to reduce misunderstandings and promote a culture of open communication. Especially in the cockpit, and cabin environments. The effective use of CRM Crew Resource Management principles and emotional intelligence all contribute to a safer and more effective and harmonious operational environment.

Decision-making. Emotional intelligence can help individuals to manage their emotions and make rational decisions, even in challenging circumstances. By developing emotional intelligence, pilots and crew members can make more informed decisions, reducing errors and promoting safety.

Effective teamwork is essential, and emotional intelligence can help to create a more cohesive and collaborative team. By developing emotional intelligence, pilots and crew members can better understand the emotions and perspectives of others, leading to more effective teamwork and improved performance.

Safety is the top priority, and emotional intelligence can help to promote a culture of safety. By developing emotional intelligence, pilots and crew members can better manage stress, communicate more effectively, make better decisions, and work together more efficiently, all of which can lead to a safer and more efficient operation. In most of the effective teams I have observed, Emotional Intelligence ranked high and was an important element in their success.

Organizations such as airlines, airports, Air Traffic Control, Group and Flight Ops as well as Space Centers can play a significant role in helping their crews develop emotional intelligence. Here are some strategies that can be employed,

Offer Training and Development Programs. Organizations can provide training and development programs that focus on emotional intelligence, including workshops, courses, and coaching. These programs can help individuals to understand and manage their emotions, communicate more effectively, and work together more efficiently. They can also help to promote a culture that values emotional intelligence and encourages individuals to develop these skills.

Create a Supportive Work Environment. Organizations can create a work environment that supports emotional intelligence development. This can be done by encouraging open communication, providing feedback, recognizing and rewarding positive behavior, and fostering a culture of teamwork and collaboration. When individuals feel supported and valued, they are more likely to develop emotional intelligence skills.

Encourage Self-Reflection and Self-Awareness. Organizations can encourage their crews to engage in self-reflection and self-awareness activities. This can include practices such as journaling, mindfulness, and regular check-ins with a mentor or coach. By promoting self-awareness, individuals can better understand their emotions, motivations, and behaviors, leading to better emotional regulation and management.

Organizations can lead by example and model emotional intelligence themselves. Leaders who demonstrate emotional intelligence skills, such as active listening, empathy, and effective communication, can inspire and motivate their crews to develop these skills themselves. By demonstrating the importance of emotional intelligence, organizations can create a culture that values these skills and encourages their development.

Regular feedback is essential to emotional intelligence development. Organizations can provide their crews with constructive feedback, both positive and negative, to help them improve their emotional intelligence skills. Feedback should be specific, actionable, and focused on behaviors, rather than personal traits. It should also be delivered in a timely manner, so individuals have a chance to reflect on their actions and make improvements.

Emotional intelligence is a lifelong learning process, and organizations can support their crews' continued learning and development by providing access to resources and opportunities to practice their skills. This can include online resources, books, peer support groups, and mentoring programs. By encouraging continued learning and growth, organizations can create a culture of continuous improvement and development.

Incorporate Emotional Intelligence into Performance Metrics. Organizations can incorporate emotional intelligence into their performance metrics, emphasizing the importance of these skills and encouraging individuals to develop them. This can be done by including emotional intelligence-related behaviors and competencies in performance evaluations and setting goals related to emotional intelligence development. By making emotional intelligence a priority in performance evaluations, organizations can ensure that individuals are held accountable for their development in this area.

How Crew and Team Members Develop Emotional Intelligence

There are several ways that pilots can develop their emotional intelligence (EI) skills:

- *Self-awareness.* The first step in developing EI is to become more aware of one's own emotions. Pilots can practice mindfulness techniques, such as meditation, to help them become more attuned to their own thoughts and feelings.
- *Self-regulation.* Once pilots are more aware of their emotions, they can practice regulating them in healthy ways. This might involve techniques such as deep breathing, progressive muscle relaxation, or cognitive restructuring.
- *Social awareness.* Pilots can also develop their social awareness by practicing active listening, observing the emotions of others, and trying to see situations from others' perspectives.
- *Relationship management.* Pilots can work on their relationship management skills by practicing effective communication, conflict resolution, and collaboration with colleagues and passengers.
- *Seek feedback.* It can also be helpful for pilots to seek feedback from others about their emotional intelligence skills. This feedback can help them to identify areas where they need to improve and to develop a plan for doing so.
- *Training and coaching.* Finally, pilots can benefit from formal training and coaching programs that are designed to help them develop their emotional intelligence skills. These programs might include workshops, online courses, or one-on-one coaching sessions with a certified coach.

By practicing these techniques and seeking out opportunities for formal training and coaching, pilots, cabin crew and industry professionals can develop their emotional intelligence skills and become more effective and resilient aviators.

Emotional intelligence (EI) can be particularly helpful in conflict resolution, as it can help pilots to navigate challenging situations with colleagues, air traffic controllers, and passengers in a way that promotes safety and positive outcomes. Here's an example of how EI can help in conflict resolution:

Imagine a situation where the captain and first officer are experiencing a miscommunication. The captain is issuing instructions to the co-pilot, but the pilot is struggling to understand them due to high workload and stress. As a result, the captain becomes frustrated and begins to argue with the colleague.

In this situation, the captain's emotional intelligence skills could come into play. Specifically, the captain could use his or her social awareness skills to recognize the emotions of the co-pilot, who is likely feeling stressed and overwhelmed too. The captain could then use his or her relationship management skills to *de-escalate* the conflict by acknowledging the pilot's feelings and taking steps to resolve the miscommunication.

For example, the captain might say something like, "I'm sorry for getting frustrated earlier. I can tell that you're under a lot of pressure, and I want to make sure we're on the same page. Can you please repeat the information so that I can confirm that I understand correctly?" This approach demonstrates empathy and understanding towards the co-pilot's feelings, while also promoting safety and effective communication.

By applying emotional intelligence skills in conflict resolution, pilots can help to reduce the risk of misunderstandings and promote positive outcomes for everyone involved. It is important that communication be respectful and professional.

Emotional intelligence can help cabin crew to manage their own emotions during conflicts, which can prevent them from becoming overly aggressive or defensive. For example, if a passenger becomes upset about a flight delay, an experienced crew member with high emotional intelligence might take a few deep breaths and try to understand the passenger's perspective before responding. This can help the pilot to always remain calm and professional, even in the face of a difficult situation.

How to Create Elite Teams and Enhance Performance.

1. Communicate regularly and openly and honestly with your leadership and teams about what resources are needed to achieve your goals.
2. Break down complex tasks into smaller more manageable steps and focus on achieving each one in order of priority.
3. Always have a clear vision of where your work is going, ensure complete commitment from leadership, and create a detailed plan.
4. Prioritize safety above all else and ensure that all team members understand their roles and responsibilities in maintaining a safe working environment.
5. Continuously review and evaluate progress, identifying any areas that need improvement and making necessary adjustments.
6. Foster a culture of collaboration, respect, and open communication among team members, regardless of their roles or backgrounds.
7. Embrace and learn from failures and setbacks, using them as opportunities to improve and refine processes.
8. Stay current with industry developments and advances in technology and incorporate them into planning and execution.
9. Always maintain a cultural focus on sustainability and environmental responsibility considering the impact on the planet and future generations.
10. Celebrate and recognize the achievements of team members and individuals, building a sense of pride and community within the project and organization.

The Spiral Training concept from Simple to Approaching Complex Tasks.

Aerial display teams train elite aviators use a method that allows for the mastery of complex maneuvers through a graduated process of learning in degrees. This approach is critical in the aviation industry, particularly for display teams who perform complex high-speed formation flying and aerial acrobatics in close proximity to one another.

The method of training involves starting with simple maneuvers and mastering each one in sequence before moving on to the next training element. This approach is akin to starting the training in the center of a swirling seashell, where the inner points are mastered before moving out to the outer training.

For instance, aviation display teams have their new trainees master the simple fly past in proximity before they attempt the next phases of angled or inverted aircraft fly past in opposite directions. By layering on the levels of complexity in a safe manner, the pilot becomes extraordinarily competent and builds confidence as the course progresses. The clearly marked stages of training provide a shared understanding of the training objectives and allow team members to work together in a cohesive manner. During this process the student learns about the actions and reactions of the other crew members of the team, which is critical for achieving synchronized maneuvers safely.

The key to training elite aviators is to start with simple maneuvers and progressively layer on complexity in a graduated manner. As we all know, aviation is an industry where safety and excellence are paramount, and this approach ensures that we achieve both.

Identify the core skills and knowledge required for the job, break them down into manageable chunks, and then build on each skill or task in sequence. By doing so, you can create a strong foundation of skills and knowledge that can be built upon over time, leading to greater competency, confidence, and success in your work.

Precision can Beat Power, and Timing can Beat Speed.

While power and speed are certainly important factors in aerial combat, they are not always the key to victory. A skilled pilot who can execute precise maneuvers and time their attacks correctly can often outmaneuver and outsmart a more powerful opponent. Consider the example of a bird of prey, such as a peregrine falcon. Despite being one of the fastest birds in the world, it is their precision and timing that make them such effective hunters. They can execute precise dives at high speeds, and time their attacks perfectly to strike their prey with deadly accuracy. The same principles can be applied to aerial combat. A skilled pilot who can execute precise maneuvers and time their attacks correctly can often outmaneuver and outsmart a more powerful opponent. It's not just about raw power or speed, but rather about being able to use your skills and knowledge to gain the upper hand. Develop your skills and knowledge and learn to anticipate your opponent's moves. By doing so, you will be able to outmaneuver and outsmart your opponents, even if they have more raw power or speed than you do. Although all those elements are important, do work on developing your precision and timing skills through practicing at optimum levels of intensity and focus. While learning to perfect the rhythm, of an oscillating pattern between intensity of focus and relaxation you will be able to navigate your mental states to ever greater degrees of effectiveness.

Psychological Safety in Workplace and Its High Importance in Company and Cultures.

Having worked in many diverse work cultures in different parts of the world, I've come to realize the value of a work culture that allows you to be comfortable and feel natural about being yourself. What I refer to here is the importance of psychological safety in the workplace and its impact on effective collaboration, problem-solving, and safe operations. For example, I have observed that when individuals feel safe to speak their minds without fear of judgment or retribution, they are more likely to contribute their unique perspectives and ideas, which can lead to better outcomes for the team and the organization.

I recommend that the leadership and stakeholders of aviation and aerospace companies work to consistently create cultures of psychological safety in their workplaces. I believe this can be achieved by,

Encouraging open communication. Leaders should actively encourage team members to speak up and share their opinions, ideas, and concerns. This can be achieved through regular team meetings, one-on-one sessions, and other communication channels.

Valuing diversity of thought. Teams should value and celebrate diversity of thought, recognizing that different perspectives and ideas can lead to more creative and effective solutions.

Listening actively. Leaders and team members should listen actively and empathetically to each other, seeking to understand each other's perspectives and concerns.

Creating a blame-free culture. Teams should strive to create a culture where individuals feel safe making mistakes and learn from them, without fear of blame or punishment. Creating a culture of psychological safety is essential for effective collaboration. By valuing and encouraging open communication and active listening, aviation and aerospace leaders and their teams can create a work environment where everyone feels safe to contribute their best ideas and work towards shared goals and best serve the needs of the industry. Psychological safety enables effective implementation of processes like the voluntary self-disclosure mechanisms between the airlines and the regulatory authorities that are vital for safe operations around the world. It allows for early detection of potential issues or hazards, enabling teams to identify and mitigate them before they turn into significant problems and safety concerns. These are integral elements in any organization's Safety Management System. It considers that human error will invariably occur and provides feedback and a mechanism for addressing issues before they become a pattern of deteriorating standards and safety concerns.

In addition, it creates an environment where individuals are comfortable admitting mistakes or errors, which is essential for continuous improvement and learning. When team members feel psychologically safe, they are more likely to be open and honest about what went wrong and how to improve.

To ensure psychological safety in your team or organization, it's essential to create an environment of trust and respect. Companies and authorities alike should encourage open communication, actively listen to employees' ideas and concerns, and avoid punishing mistakes or failures. This creates a culture where team members feel valued and respected, and it fosters a sense of shared responsibility for achieving the organizational goals.

Training elite level teams for top performance starts with a clear focus on the mission and a commitment to excellence in every aspect of our work.

It's important to build teams that are composed of individuals who are passionate about their work and committed to achieving the mission. Look for people who are not only skilled but also have the right attitude, work ethic, and team-oriented mindset. We believe that the whole is greater than the sum of its parts, and we strive to create a culture of mutual respect, trust, and collaboration.

Successful teams place a high value on structured training that builds skills in a progressive and systematic way, starting with the basics and gradually increasing the level of difficulty. Ensure that each team member has a solid foundation of knowledge and skill before moving on to more advanced techniques and maneuvers. This approach not only helps to develop individual competence but also fosters team cohesion and trust. Effective communication is essential to high performance. Display teams, for example, practice clear and concise communication in all aspects of their work, from mission planning to executing maneuvers in the air. They use standardized procedures and terminology to ensure everyone is on the same page and encourage open and honest feedback so that they can continuously improve performance.

Professionalism and Airmanship

As pilots, you already have many skills that are essential for success - technical knowledge, attention to detail, and a dedication to safety, to name a few. But when it comes to performing during intense workload situations, such as during an emergency or a challenging flight, it's important to develop additional skills that will help you stay calm, focused, and engaged with your passengers and crew. One of the most important performance skills for aviators is confidence. When you're in the cockpit, your passengers are looking to you for reassurance that everything is under control. This means projecting an air of calm and competence, even if you're feeling anxious or uncertain. Practice deep breathing and visualization techniques to help calm your nerves and stay focused on the task at hand. Maintain postures of assurance, not arrogance or showiness but a classy professionalism that instills confidence in all who are along with you for the operation. Try to stay engaged with your passengers and crew at key moments throughout the flight. This means making eye contact, asking questions, and taking the time to listen to their concerns and feedback. By creating a sense of personal connection, you can help build trust and confidence among your team. Belief is a powerful force that can shape our thoughts, actions, and outcomes. When we believe in ourselves and our abilities, we are more likely to perform at our best and achieve our goals. On the other hand, when we doubt ourselves or our abilities, we may struggle to perform at our full potential.

As aviators, it's important to cultivate a strong sense of belief in ourselves and our abilities. This means having confidence in our training and experience, and trusting in our ability to handle any situation that may arise during a flight.

One way to build belief is through positive self-talk. This means consciously replacing negative or self-doubting thoughts with positive, affirming statements. For example, if you find yourself thinking, "I'm not sure if I can handle this," try reframing that thought into something like, "I am trained and prepared to handle this."

Another way to build belief is through visualization. This means mentally rehearsing a successful outcome in your mind before it happens. For example, before a flight, you might visualize yourself completing the flight safely and confidently, and handling any challenges that may arise.

It's important to note that building belief takes time and effort. It's not something that happens overnight, but rather a process of consistent practice and reinforcement. With patience and dedication, you can cultivate a strong sense of belief in yourself and your abilities as an aviator. By repeating positive affirmations and adding in "I feel it" you add an emotional component that will help it stick in your mind.

Autosuggestion

Autosuggestion is a useful technique that can help you to achieve your goals and improve your performance as an aviator. Autosuggestion is the process of repeating positive affirmations to yourself in order to reinforce positive beliefs and attitudes.

The key to effective autosuggestion is to use positive, affirming statements that are specific to your goals and desires. For example, if your goal is to improve your performance during takeoff, you might repeat to yourself something like, 'I am confident and skilled during takeoff, and I am able to handle any challenges that may arise.

When practicing autosuggestion, it's important to use visualization techniques to reinforce the positive statements. This means visualizing yourself performing the desired behavior or achieving the desired outcome. For example, you might visualize yourself taking off smoothly and confidently, and handling any issues that arise with ease and competence. The key to effective autosuggestion is repetition. You should repeat your positive affirmations and visualizations to yourself daily, ideally multiple times per day. Your positive statements should be in the present tense indicating that the desired outcome is already manifest. The more you repeat the positive statements and visualize the desired outcomes, the more deeply ingrained they will become in your subconscious mind.

It's important to note that while autosuggestion can be a powerful tool for achieving your goals, it is not a magic solution. It requires consistent practice and effort, and it may take time to see results. By proceeding with patience and dedication, you can use autosuggestion to reinforce positive beliefs and attitudes and improve your performance as an aviator. Your thinking stream is always flowing so you might as well make it a positive stream. The alternative is not so good, and it's important to understand how negative thought forms, such as fear or anxiety, can impact their mental and physical states during operations. Negative thought forms can trigger a stress response in the body, which can result in physiological changes such as increased heart rate and respiration, decreased cognitive performance, and decreased ability to make effective decisions. Negative thought forms such as pessimism and self-doubt can have a detrimental effect on mental and physical health, as well as overall performance and success. Negative thought forms can lead to a cycle of negative self-talk and self-sabotage, which can limit aviators' potential and create unnecessary barriers to success.

By recognizing and challenging negative thought forms, aviators can develop a more positive and adaptive mindset that allows them to perform at their best even under stressful conditions. This can involve techniques such as cognitive reframing, positive self-talk, and visualization exercises, which can help to rewire the brain to respond more effectively to stressors. By understanding the influence of thought forms on our mental and physical states, aviators can develop a more resilient and adaptive mindset that enables them to perform their duties safely and effectively, even under challenging conditions.

Visualization

To become good at visualization takes time and practice, but there are several techniques that can be helpful in developing this skill. Here are some strategies that you can try:

Practice visualization regularly. One of the most important things you can do to become a master visualizer is to practice visualization regularly. Set aside time each day to visualize a specific image or scenario, and focus on building vivid, detailed mental images.

Use all your senses. To create a truly immersive visualization experience, engage all your senses. Try to imagine the sights, sounds, smells, tastes, and textures associated with your mental image or scenario.

Focus on details. Pay close attention to the details of your mental images. Visualize the texture of objects, the colors of the scene, and the shapes of the objects. The more specific and detailed you can make your mental images, the more immersive and engaging they will be.

Use guided visualizations. Guided visualizations can be helpful in developing your visualization skills. Listen to a guided visualization recording and follow along with the instructions to build your visualization skills.

Create a vision board. A vision board is a physical representation of your goals and aspirations. Create a board with pictures and words that represent the things you want to achieve or experience. Spend time looking at your vision board each day and use it to help you visualize your goals.

Exercise

Here's an exercise that can help you develop their visualization skills,

1. Find a quiet, comfortable space where you won't be disturbed for a few minutes.
2. Close your eyes and take a few deep breaths to relax your body and clear your mind.
3. Choose a simple image or scene to visualize. For example, you could imagine a beach, a forest, or a waterfall. Start with something simple and easy to visualize.
4. Begin to build the image in your mind, using all your senses to create a vivid and immersive mental picture. Imagine the colors, textures, and shapes of the scene, as well as any sounds, smells, or sensations associated with it.
5. Hold the image in your mind for a few minutes, focusing on the details and allowing yourself to fully immerse yourself in the scene.
6. When you're ready, slowly open your eyes and take a few more deep breaths.
7. Take a few moments to reflect on your experience. How vivid was your mental image? Did you notice any areas where you struggled to create a clear mental picture? What could you do differently next time to improve your visualization skills?

Mental images are the visual representations that we create in our minds. These mental images can be based on real-life experiences or completely imagined scenarios, and they are created through the process of visualization. By practicing visualization exercises, such as the one I just provided, aviators and astronauts and flight crews can develop their ability to create and hold clear mental images in their minds. Thought forms refer to the energy patterns that are created by our thoughts and emotions. When we think a thought or feel an emotion, we are creating a vibrational energy that can affect our mental, emotional, and physical states. By becoming more aware of our thought forms, we can begin to consciously direct our thoughts and emotions towards positive outcomes, such as improved performance and well-being.

Thought patterns are the recurring mental habits and tendencies that shape our thinking and behavior. For example, if we tend to dwell on negative thoughts, this can create a negative thought pattern that can impact our overall mindset and outlook on life. By becoming more aware of our thought patterns, we can begin to identify and challenge negative thinking habits and replace them with more positive and productive thought patterns. By understanding and developing these mental skills, you can become more effective at managing your thoughts and emotions and creating positive mental states that support optimal performance and well-being.

These mental skills are critical for aviation professionals because they directly impact their ability to perform their jobs safely, effectively, and efficiently. Here are some examples of how these mental skills are important in aviation.

Pilots need to be able to focus their attention on multiple tasks at once, such as monitoring instruments, communicating with air traffic control, and scanning for other aircraft. They also need to be able to sustain their attention over long periods of time, such as during long flights or during critical phases of flight. Pilots need to be able to remember and recall vast amounts of information, such as procedures, checklists, and regulations. They also need to be able to recall information quickly and accurately in emergency situations. They need to be able to analyze complex situations and make informed decisions quickly and accurately. For example, if an instrument malfunctions, the pilot needs to be able to assess the situation, determine the appropriate course of action, and execute that action safely and efficiently. Flight

Deck Crew need to be able to think creatively and adapt to changing circumstances. For example, if weather conditions change unexpectedly, the pilot needs to be able to adjust their flight plan and make decisions quickly to ensure the safety of the flight. Emotional regulation, pilots need to be able to manage their emotions and remain calm under pressure. For example, if an emergency occurs, the pilot needs to be able to stay focused and make clear decisions, even in a stressful and chaotic environment.

Pilots need to be able to bounce back from setbacks and adapt to changing circumstances. For example, if a flight is delayed or cancelled, the pilot needs to be able to adjust their plans and stay motivated and focused. All these are important mental skills to learn and develop through training, practice and application.

Metacognition

Metacognition is the process of thinking about thinking. It involves being aware of your own thoughts and thought processes, monitoring them, and adjusting as needed. Essentially, it's thinking about how you think. It can help you become more aware of your own thinking patterns and identify when you might be making errors or overlooking important details. It can also help you regulate your emotions.

So, how can you apply metacognition in your work? First, start by becoming more aware of your own thought processes. Take a moment to reflect on how you approach tasks and problem-solving. Are there patterns or tendencies that you notice? Once you're aware of these patterns, you can start to adjust them.

After completing a task or solving a problem, take some time to reflect on what went well and what could be improved. This can help you identify areas where you need to focus your attention in the future. This refers to our approach to the feedback loop of continuous improvement. What went well? What did not go so well? And what I do better next time? Metacognition can help you become more effective at learning and skill-building. By being aware of your own thinking processes and identifying areas for improvement, you can develop more targeted and efficient strategies for learning and practicing new skills. Being aware of your own thinking patterns and adjusting as needed makes you a more effective problem-solver and better equipped to handle your work.

Here are some strategies for Metacognition,

Effective metacognitive strategies include:

- *Planning.* Setting clear goals, defining the steps required to achieve them, and monitoring progress towards these goals.
- *Monitoring.* Being aware of your own thinking and learning process, recognizing when you are making mistakes or

encountering difficulties, and adjusting your approach accordingly.

- *Evaluation.* Reflecting on your learning experience, identifying what worked well and what did not, and using this information to improve your approach in the future.
- *Regulation.* Regulating your own learning process by managing your attention, selecting appropriate learning strategies, and adapting your approach as needed.
- *Feedback.* Seeking feedback from others, evaluating the feedback you receive, and using it to make improvements in your learning and thinking process.

Self-Regulated Learning (SRL)

I want to go a bit further and discuss self-regulated learning, which is the process of taking control of your own learning by setting goals, monitoring your progress, and adjusting your learning strategies as needed. Since when it comes to wellbeing and mental training, many of the airlines, and aviation organizations around the world do not have structured courses in place that are adequate to address the needs of professionals. When it comes to learning, we often rely on external factors such as teachers, textbooks, and lectures to guide us. However, self-regulated learning is about taking responsibility for your own learning and using internal resources to improve your skills and knowledge. One of the key components of self-regulated learning is goal setting. This means setting specific and achievable goals for yourself, and identifying the steps you need to take to achieve those goals. By setting goals, you give yourself direction and purpose, and can measure your progress along the way.

Let's look at the aspect of self-regulated learning known as monitoring. This means keeping track of your progress, and reflecting on your learning to identify areas where you need to improve. In the process of monitoring your progress, you identify what's working well and what needs to change and adjust your learning strategies accordingly. In short, self-regulated learning is about using effective learning strategies. This means identifying the strategies that work best for you and using them consistently to achieve your goals. Effective learning strategies can include things like active reading, note-taking, and practice testing.

How can you start practicing self-regulated learning? One technique is to start with small, achievable goals, and gradually work your way up to more challenging ones. Set a goal for yourself, and then break it down into smaller steps that you can tackle one at a time. By doing this, you can build your confidence and motivation, and develop the skills you need to take control of your own learning.

Self-regulated learning is a process, not a destination. It's about developing the skills and habits that will help you become a lifelong learner. By setting goals, monitoring your progress, and using effective learning strategies, you can take control of your own learning.

Cognitive Restructuring

Cognitive restructuring can be used to change negative thought patterns into positive ones. This technique can be especially useful for individuals who struggle with anxiety, stress, or self-doubt.

The basic idea behind cognitive restructuring is to identify negative or unhelpful thoughts that are contributing to a negative emotional state or negative behavior. Once these negative thoughts have been identified, the individual can work to challenge and change them by looking for evidence that contradicts them, re-framing the thought in a more positive or neutral way, or coming up with more balanced and realistic thoughts that consider the full picture.

For example, a passenger who experiences anxiety about flying may have a negative thought like "I'm going to crash and die." This thought can be challenged by looking for evidence to the contrary, such as statistics on the safety of air travel, or by re-framing the thought in a more positive or neutral way, such as "I'm going to take all the necessary precautions and trust in the expertise of the pilots and crew."

Cognitive restructuring can also be helpful for changing negative self-talk that contributes to low self-esteem or self-doubt. For example, an airman who is struggling with self-doubt may have a negative thought like "I'm not good enough to handle this situation." This thought can be challenged by looking for evidence to the contrary, such as past successes or positive feedback from colleagues, or by re-framing the thought in a more positive or neutral way, such as "I have the skills and experience necessary to handle this situation."

One example of a structured cognitive restructuring technique is the ABCDE model developed by Dr. Albert Ellis, the founder of Rational Emotive Behavioral Therapy (REBT). The ABCDE model is a simple framework for identifying and challenging irrational beliefs that can lead to negative emotions and behaviors.

A stands for Activating event, which refers to a specific situation or event that triggers negative thoughts and emotions.

B stands for Belief, which is the negative thought or belief that arises from the activating event. This belief can be irrational or unrealistic.

C stands for Consequence, which refers to the negative emotional and behavioral responses that result from the negative belief.

D stands for Dispute, which involves questioning and challenging the negative belief using rational and evidence-based thinking.

E stands for Effective new belief, which involves replacing the negative belief with a more rational and positive belief.

For example, let's say a trainee pilot has made a mistake during a flight and starts to think, "I am a terrible pilot and I'm going to get fired." In this case, the activating event is the mistake made during the flight, the negative belief is "I am a terrible pilot and I'm going to get fired," and the consequence is feelings of anxiety and self-doubt. Using the ABCDE model, the pilot can challenge the negative belief by disputing it with evidence-based thinking. They can ask themselves, "Is this belief based on fact or is it an overgeneralization? Have I made mistakes before and not gotten fired? What evidence is there that I am a competent pilot?" By disputing the negative belief, the student pilot can replace it with a more rational and positive belief, such as "I made a mistake, but I am still a competent pilot, and I can learn from this experience." This can lead to a more positive emotional and behavioral response.

Exposure Therapy

Exposure therapy is a type of cognitive-behavioral therapy that involves gradually exposing a person to the feared situation or object in a controlled and safe environment. It is often used to help individuals overcome anxiety disorders, phobias, and post-traumatic stress disorder (PTSD). In the context of military pilots who have survived a near-fatal incident or close call-in combat, exposure therapy can be a highly effective treatment option.

When a military pilot experiences a traumatic event, such as surviving a near-fatal incident while flying or near-death experience in combat, it can lead to feelings of fear, anxiety, and apprehension that can significantly impact their ability to perform their job. Exposure therapy helps to reduce the intensity of these feelings by gradually exposing the pilot to the situation or object that triggers the fear response.

The therapy can be conducted in various ways, including in live exposure, which involves real-life exposure to the feared situation or object, or imaginal exposure, which involves exposure to the feared situation or object in the person's imagination. The goal is to help the airman learn to cope with the anxiety and fear associated with the traumatic event and to develop effective coping strategies.

For example, a military pilot who has survived a near-fatal crash may experience intense fear and apprehension when flying again. Through exposure therapy, the pilot would be gradually exposed to the elements of flying that trigger their fear, such as turbulence or steep high G turns, in a safe and controlled environment. Over time, the pilot would learn to tolerate these experiences and develop effective coping strategies, such as deep breathing or positive self-talk, to manage their anxiety.

Exposure therapy has been shown to be highly effective in treating PTSD and anxiety disorders in military populations. It is a structured and evidence-based technique that can help military pilots overcome the fear and apprehension associated with a traumatic event and get back to performing their job with confidence and resilience.

Let's look at an example, if an airman has developed a fear of flying after experiencing a close call during a combat mission, the exposure therapy may involve starting with simulators or virtual reality training, which simulate the cockpit environment and the experience of flying.

As the pilot becomes more comfortable with the simulator or virtual reality training, they can progress to actual flights in a safe and controlled environment, such as with an experienced flight instructor or in a dual-control aircraft. The pilot can then gradually increase their exposure to more challenging flights or maneuvers until they are able to fly with confidence and without experiencing the same level of fear or apprehension. Through this gradual process of exposure and desensitization, the pilot's brain can learn to associate the once-fearful stimuli with a sense of safety and control, ultimately leading to a reduction in fear and anxiety.

Progressive Muscle Relaxation

Progressive muscle relaxation is a technique that can be helpful for military aviators and astronauts who experience stress and tension related to their work. The technique involves tensing and then relaxing muscle groups in a specific order, which can help to release tension and promote relaxation throughout the body. This can be particularly helpful for individuals who experience physical symptoms of stress, such as muscle tension or headaches. It works by systematically tensing and then relaxing different muscle groups in your body. By doing this, you can learn to recognize when your muscles are tense and consciously relax them, which can help you to feel more relaxed overall.

Exercise

To practice Progressive Muscle Relaxation, you'll want to start by finding a quiet and comfortable place to sit or lie down. Begin by tensing the muscles in your toes and feet, holding the tension for about 10 seconds, and then releasing the tension and relaxing those muscles completely. You can then move on to the muscles in your calves, thighs, buttocks, and so on, working your way up your body.

As you work through each muscle group, make sure to take slow, deep breaths, inhaling deeply and then exhaling slowly as you release the tension in each muscle group. You may want to imagine that you are breathing in relaxation and breathing out tension, letting go of any stress or anxiety that you may be feeling.

One important thing to keep in mind as you practice Progressive Muscle Relaxation is to focus on the physical sensations that you are experiencing in each muscle group, rather than getting caught up in your thoughts or worries. By paying attention to your body, you can learn to recognize when you are feeling tense and use this technique to help you relax. Over time, with practice, Progressive Muscle Relaxation can become a valuable tool in your stress management toolkit, helping you to feel more relaxed and calmer, even in challenging situations.

Biofeedback

Biofeedback is a technique that involves using instruments to monitor the physiological responses of the body, such as heart rate, breathing, and muscle tension, and then providing real-time feedback to the individual on their body's responses. By using this technique, individuals can learn to control their physiological responses and improve their overall physical and mental performance.

For military aviators and astronauts, biofeedback can be a valuable tool for managing stress and improving cognitive performance. Here are the key aspects of biofeedback.

Biofeedback typically involves the use of sensors or instruments that measure physiological responses, such as heart rate monitors, electromyography (EMG) sensors to measure muscle tension, and electroencephalography (EEG) sensors to measure brainwave activity. Once the instruments are in place, the individual can receive real-time feedback on their physiological responses. This feedback can be provided in a variety of forms, such as visual displays, sounds, or vibrations. To use biofeedback effectively, individuals typically need to learn relaxation techniques, such as deep breathing or progressive muscle relaxation. By combining these techniques with biofeedback, individuals can learn to control their physiological responses and achieve a state of relaxation even in high-pressure situations. The benefits of biofeedback for military aviators and astronauts include improved stress management, enhanced cognitive performance, and better overall physical and mental health.

Rest and Recovery

One of the most important aspects of achieving elite level performance and maintaining it is recovery. It is not just about pushing yourself to the limit during training or operations, but also taking the time to rest, recover, and recharge.

Aviators and astronauts are exposed to unique stressors that can take a toll on both their physical and mental health. The high altitude, exposure to cabin pressures, zero gravity, long hours, and intense workload can lead to exhaustion and burnout if proper recovery measures are not taken.

Some effective recovery techniques include getting adequate sleep, maintaining a healthy diet, engaging in relaxation techniques like yoga or meditation, taking time off for vacations or hobbies, and seeking support from peers, friends, and family.

Sleep is a critical component of recovery. It allows the body to repair and restore itself and supports cognitive functioning and memory consolidation. Aim for 7-9 hours of sleep each night and prioritize a consistent sleep schedule even during periods of travel or shift work where possible. Nutrition is also an important factor in recovery. Eating a balanced diet rich in whole foods can provide the necessary nutrients for optimal recovery and performance. Proper hydration is also key, as dehydration can cause fatigue and impair cognitive functioning. Relaxation techniques like yoga, meditation, and deep breathing exercises can also be effective in reducing stress and promoting relaxation. These techniques have been shown to lower cortisol levels, decrease blood pressure, and improve mood and cognitive functioning.

Taking time off for vacations, spending time with family and hobbies is also important for recovery. This allows for a mental break from work, which can help to reduce stress and promote overall well-being. Engaging in activities you enjoy can also promote feelings of happiness and fulfillment, which can contribute to better overall mental health. Seeking support from peers, friends, and family is essential for maintaining mental health and promoting recovery. Having a strong support system can help individuals cope with stress and feel less isolated. Additionally, seeking professional help from a therapist or counselor can be beneficial for those experiencing significant stress or mental health challenges.

Overall, recovery is a crucial aspect of achieving elite level performance for aviation and aerospace professionals. Prioritizing rest, relaxation, and support can help individuals to maintain optimal physical and mental health and achieve their professional goals. Do not suffer in silence, talk with someone. In order to maintain a top level, high intensity performance it is essential to rest and recover well at correct intervals. Light exercise, such as walking or cycling, increases blood flow to the muscles and can help to flush out metabolic waste products that can build up during periods of intense activity. This can help to reduce muscle soreness and stiffness and improve overall mobility. Foam rolling, or self-myofascial release, involves using a foam roller or similar tool to apply pressure to specific muscles and soft tissues to release tension and promote relaxation. This can help to improve circulation and reduce muscle tightness and soreness.

Stretching is another important active recovery technique that can help to improve flexibility and mobility, reduce muscle soreness, and prevent injury. Stretching can be done in a variety of ways, including static stretching, dynamic stretching, and PNF stretching. Static stretching involves holding a stretch for a period, while dynamic stretching involves moving through a range of motion in a controlled manner. PNF stretching is about contracting and relaxing muscles while stretching to improve range of motion. Active recovery techniques should be used in conjunction with other recovery strategies, such as rest, hydration, and nutrition, to achieve optimal results. By incorporating these techniques into your recovery routine, you can help to reduce muscle soreness and fatigue, improve flexibility and mobility, and ultimately optimize your performance. Massage can also help to increase blood flow and oxygenation, reduce inflammation and muscle tension, and promote relaxation and stress reduction. It can also help to improve range of motion and flexibility, which can be particularly beneficial for aviation and aerospace professionals who spend long periods of time in cramped and confined spaces. Massage is the manipulation of soft tissues to reduce muscle tension, increase blood flow, and promote relaxation. Massage therapy can help alleviate soreness, stiffness, and inflammation, which are common after intense physical activity. There are different types of massage techniques that can be used, including Swedish massage, deep tissue massage, and sports massage. Each type of massage targets different muscle groups and tissues and has specific benefits for the body. Swedish massage is a gentle form of massage that uses long strokes, kneading, and circular movements to promote relaxation and improve circulation. Deep tissue massage, on the other hand, uses slow, deep pressure to target the deeper layers of muscle and connective tissue, which can help alleviate chronic muscle pain and stiffness. Sports massage is a type of massage that is specifically designed for athletes and can help improve flexibility, prevent injuries, and enhance performance.

Massage therapy can be a beneficial recovery strategy, particularly after long flights or intense training sessions. It can help reduce muscle soreness, improve circulation, and promote relaxation and stress relief.

Integrity and Professional Excellence

I have always tried to embody the principles of integrity and professionalism. To me, these are not just buzzwords or abstract concepts, but rather they are the foundation upon which personal excellence is built.

What do I mean when I talk about integrity and professionalism? To me, integrity means doing what is right, even when no one is watching. It means being honest, transparent, and accountable in all your actions and decisions. And it means treating others with respect, fairness, and compassion.

Professionalism is about having a strong work ethic, a commitment to quality, and a willingness to go above and beyond in pursuit of excellence. It means being reliable, punctual, and organized, and it means being able to communicate effectively with others.

Why are integrity and professionalism so important for personal excellence? Well, for one thing, they are essential for building trust and credibility with others. If people don't believe that you are honest, reliable, and competent, they are unlikely to want to work with you or do business with you. And if you don't have a reputation for integrity and professionalism, it can be difficult to attract and retain the best talent, customers, and partners. Even more importantly, I believe that integrity and professionalism are essential for personal fulfillment and happiness. When you live your life with integrity, you can be proud of who you are and what you stand for. And when you approach your work with professionalism, you can take pride in your accomplishments and feel a sense of satisfaction from doing your best.

Of course, living a life of integrity and professionalism is not always easy. There will be times when you are faced with difficult decisions, when it may be tempting to take shortcuts or compromise your values. It is during these times that your true character is revealed. It is during these times that you may demonstrate your commitment to integrity and professionalism, and to show that you are a person of true character and strength.

How can you cultivate a commitment to integrity and professionalism in your own life? I have a few suggestions,

Be honest with yourself and with others. Don't try to hide your mistakes or cover up your shortcomings. Instead, own up to your failures, and use them as opportunities for growth and learning. Be reliable and consistent in your actions. If you say you are going to do something, follow through on your commitments. Be punctual, and respect other people's time. Practice being respectful and compassionate towards others. Treat everyone you meet with dignity and kindness, regardless of their position or status. Always be willing to lend a helping hand when someone is in need.

Never stop striving for excellence. Don't be satisfied with mediocrity or complacency. Instead, push yourself to be the best that you can be, and never stop learning and growing. I want to emphasize that living a life of integrity and professionalism is not just about being successful in your career or achieving your goals. It is about being a person of true character and substance, someone who is respected and admired by others for their honesty, reliability, and commitment to excellence.

I believe it is hugely important to lead by example. As a leader, whether it's in your family, your community, or your workplace, you have a responsibility to set the tone and to model the behaviors that you expect from others. When one is promoted to captain or commander of a mission, if you want your team to be honest, transparent, and accountable, you need to be those things yourself. If you want your colleagues to be reliable and punctual, you need to be that way yourself. And if you want your organization to be committed to excellence, you need to embody that commitment in everything that you do. When asking people to do things, you should stop, and think is it something that I would be prepared to do. I've always believed that leadership is not about a title or a position, it's about a mindset and a way of being. And when you lead with integrity and professionalism, you inspire others to do the same. You create a culture of excellence, where everyone is motivated to do their best and to contribute to the success of the team. When you get your command or if you are in a leadership position, take this responsibility seriously. Be the kind of leader that you would want to follow, and always remember that your actions speak louder than your words.

Living a life of integrity and professionalism is not always easy, and there will be times when you face challenges or obstacles that test your commitment to these principles. When you stay true to your values and your beliefs, even in the face of adversity, you will find that the rewards are truly worth it. You will earn the respect of others, and most importantly you will respect yourself, you will build strong relationships and lasting friendships, and you will feel a sense of satisfaction and fulfillment that comes from living a life of purpose and meaning. Stay true to yourself, stay true to your values, and to always strive for personal excellence in everything that you do.

Qualities of Excellence - Courage and Persistence in the Face of Adversity.

One of the most important qualities that any person can possess is courage. The courage to stand up for what you believe in, to face your fears head-on, and to persist in the face of adversity. I know you have faced challenges and obstacles in your life. You may have faced financial difficulties, health problems, or personal setbacks. These are a part of life. I'm here to tell you that it is not the adversity that defines you, but rather how you respond to it. As I mentioned earlier, true courage is not the lack of fear, but rather the willingness to face it and to act despite it. It is the ability to push through your doubts and uncertainties, and to persist in the pursuit of your goals and dreams.

Persistence is key. Success is not something that happens overnight. It is the result of hard work, determination, and the willingness to keep pushing forward even when the going gets tough.

During my many years in the industry, I saw firsthand the power of courage and persistence in the face of adversity. Our teams faced incredible challenges over the years, from emergency situations, incidents, accidents, terrorist attacks, and even personal and touching family circumstances. I've seen emergency response teams rise to the occasion and deal with very impactful and some traumatic things. I've lost colleagues in the field and seen the impact of tragedy. However, despite these obstacles, the resilient folks never gave up. They never lost sight of their mission or their commitment to their mission and goals. That same spirit of courage and persistence is just as relevant in our personal lives as it is in our professional lives. Whether you're striving to achieve a personal goal, overcome a difficult challenge, or make a positive difference in the world, the key is to keep moving forward, one step at a time. Let me be clear here, persistence does not mean stubbornness. It's important to be willing to adapt and adjust your approach as needed, to learn from your mistakes, and to seek help and guidance when necessary. However, at the same time, you must never lose sight of your ultimate goal, and you must always be willing to put in the hard work and effort required to achieve it. Action is required.

As you face the many challenges and obstacles that come your way cultivate the spirit of courage and persistence within yourselves. Embrace your fears and use them as a source of motivation rather than a source of paralysis. Convert that energy into excitement and readiness rather than a hindrance. Keep pushing forward, even when it feels like the odds are against you. Personal excellence comes not from avoiding adversity, but from facing it head-on and emerging stronger on the other side. Courage and persistence are about living a meaningful and purposeful life and making a positive difference in the world. Cultivate these qualities within yourselves and keep your focus on the bigger picture, and to use your courage and persistence to create positive change in your own life and in the lives of those around you.

Developing Courage

Courage is essential in your line of work. It takes great courage to venture into the unknown, to take on difficult challenges, and to risk your lives for the sake of exploration and discovery. Courage is not just about facing danger; it's also about facing uncertainty, doubt, and fear. It takes courage to persevere in the face of adversity and to stay true to your values and principles. You can foster courage by facing your fears and embracing uncertainty. True courage is not the absence of fear but the ability to act despite it.

Fear is a natural response to new and challenging situations, and it is not something to be ashamed of. We all pass through different states of mind each day, and some are resourceful and others limiting and doubtful.

In order to develop courage, it is important to practice facing your fears head-on. Think of specific situations that make you feel anxious or scared and actively seek them out. For example, practicing emergency procedures or simulating difficult scenarios during training can help you become more confident in your abilities and reduce the impact of fear on your performance. Many professionals become very competent in the flight simulators and benefit from the training in realistic flight-like conditions.

Courage is not just important for your missions in space, in the air or facing heavy stressful days at ATC but also for your personal lives. Take this opportunity to reflect on areas where you may be holding back due to fear and commit to taking small steps towards facing those fears. With practice and perseverance, you will find that you can achieve more than you ever thought possible.

When it comes to courage, there are three things that I want to emphasize.

You need to know your 'why.' What is your purpose? Why are you doing what you're doing? When you have a strong sense of purpose, it gives you the courage to face any obstacle. Take a few minutes to think about your 'why.' Write it down and always keep it with you.

Just like you condition your body at the gym, you need to condition your mind for courage. This means exposing yourself to challenging situations, facing your fears, and pushing through discomfort. When you do this consistently, you'll find that courage becomes a habit.

Surround yourself with people who inspire you. As the saying goes, you are the average of the five people you spend the most time with. Make sure you're spending time with people who encourage and motivate you. If you can't find those people in your immediate circle, seek out mentors, coaches, and communities that align with your values and goals. Be in the company of supportive individuals who can encourage you and remind you of your strengths. Foster cultures of positive encouragement in your line of work develop the trust that your fellow crew members are there to support you, and that you support them.

Don't Big It Up, Press on with Optimum Performance Focus.

I have come across many aviation professionals who have faced adversity and triumphed through the power of purpose, conditioning, and community. Whether you're a pilot navigating through turbulent weather, an astronaut exploring the unknown depths of space, or a ground crew member dealing with a high-pressure situation, courage is what drives you forward. You must learn to embrace fear and use it as a catalyst to propel you forward. Numerous aviation professionals I've worked with have developed the ability to transform nervous energy into excitement within their mindset, utilizing it as fuel to propel them forward and enhance their performance to an elite level. This reframing technique enables them to maintain a heightened state of alertness and sharpness, allowing them to stay focused and adaptable in the face of high-pressure situations. By channeling their nervous energy in a positive direction, they can utilize it as a catalyst for courage and a means for achieving their goals. This powerful shift in mindset can be a game changer for aviation professionals, enabling them to achieve their objectives with a sense of confidence, determination, and purpose.

A mindset shift that can make all the difference in your performance and success in the aviation industry. It's the idea of approaching a task or challenge with the mindset of reducing it to a more manageable level, rather than "bigging it up."

When we perceive a task as too significant or insurmountable, it can be overwhelming and paralyzing, leading to anxiety and stress. It can even cause us to procrastinate or avoid the task altogether, which only adds to our stress levels and creates a negative cycle of inaction or inhibited performance.

The aviation industry is one of the most demanding fields out there, with critical safety concerns and tight deadlines. It's easy to feel the weight of these responsibilities, but it's essential to remember that our perception of these tasks can be a significant determinant of our ability to handle them.

One of the keys to success in any field is to approach tasks with a growth mindset. This means believing that our abilities are not fixed and that we can continually improve and grow in our skills and knowledge. When we approach a task with a growth mindset, we are more likely to view it as an opportunity to learn and develop, rather than a test of our fixed abilities.

When we "big up" a task or challenge, we are essentially telling ourselves that we are not up to the task, that we don't have the skills or knowledge required to succeed. This kind of self-talk can be incredibly limiting and self-defeating. Instead, we need to focus on the progress we've made so far, the skills and knowledge we've acquired, and the support we have around us to help us tackle the task at hand. It's an old adage that whether you think you can or think you can't your right.

Another essential technique is to reframe our perception of nervousness or anxiety as excitement. Many top performers in the aviation industry have learned to use the energy of nervousness to fuel their performance, rather than allowing it to undermine their confidence and focus. By reframing this feeling as excitement, we can tap into the positive energy and focus it towards achieving our goals.

When we approach a task with a sense of gratitude and appreciation, we are more likely to approach it with a positive and motivated mindset, rather than a negative and defeated one.

Approaching tasks in the aviation industry with a growth mindset, breaking them down into smaller, manageable steps, reframing nervousness as excitement, and cultivating a sense of gratitude can make all the difference in your performance and success. Practice these techniques and focus on the progress you're making, rather than the challenges you're facing. With the right mindset and approach, there's no limit to what you can achieve in this exciting and critical field.

These issues affect all kinds of pilots who operate in different arenas. For example, a research study (Bauer, H., Herbig, B., 2019) investigated work stressors and resources and their association with work engagement, subjective well-being, and energy levels in European Helicopter emergency medical services (HEMS) pilots. HEM pilots' work is highly demanding and safety critical, and much more data is needed to be gathered on occupational stress and strain symptoms.[13]

The Discipline of Professional Excellence

Discipline is another crucial quality that you must possess as astronauts and flight crews. Discipline is the ability to stay focused on your goals and to maintain a high level of performance even in the face of distractions and temptations. Discipline requires self-control, determination, and the willingness to do what needs to be done, even when it's difficult or unpleasant. I encourage you to cultivate your discipline by setting clear goals, developing good habits, and maintaining a strong sense of purpose. Discipline is the foundation upon which all success is built. It's the ability to do what needs to be done, even when you don't feel like doing it.

To truly excel in your field, you must be disciplined in every aspect of your work. This means having the discipline to show up on time, to stay focused and engaged throughout the day, to constantly strive to improve your skills and knowledge, and to push yourself beyond your comfort zone. In the aviation and aerospace industry, discipline is not just a nice-to-have attribute, it's an absolute necessity. The slightest lapse in discipline can have consequences for safety. That's why it's so important to develop and maintain a high level of professional discipline.

How do you cultivate discipline? One of the keys is to establish a routine and stick to it. Plan your flight and fly your plan. This means setting clear goals, creating a plan of action, and following through on that plan, day in and day out. Developing habits of following through in the best way you can.

Another important aspect of discipline is accountability. Hold yourself accountable for your actions and take responsibility for your mistakes. Learn from your failures and use them as an opportunity to grow and improve.

Always keep in mind the bigger picture. Remember why you got into this field in the first place and keep that vision at the forefront of your mind. Stay focused on your goals, and let your discipline guide you towards achieving them.

Discipline is an essential ingredient for success in any profession, but particularly so in the aviation and aerospace industry. By establishing a routine, holding yourself accountable, and keeping your eye on the bigger picture, you can cultivate the discipline you need to excel in your field.

Commitment

When it comes to achieving personal excellence, there are few qualities more important than discipline and commitment. These are the qualities that allow us to stay focused on our goals, to push through our fears and doubts, and to stay on track even when the going gets tough. I know that discipline and commitment are not always easy. They require hard work, sacrifice, and a willingness to put in the time and effort required to achieve your goals. However, the rewards of discipline and commitment are well worth the effort.

In many of the world-class teams I have worked with, discipline and commitment were essential to our success. We had to be disciplined in our training, our strategies and tactics, and our execution of the mission. We had to be committed to our fellow colleagues and to the values that we held in common. Whether you're striving to achieve a personal goal, to improve your health and fitness, or to make a positive difference in the world, the key is to stay disciplined and committed to your vision.

What does discipline and commitment really mean, and how can you cultivate these qualities within yourself? Let me share a few thoughts on this.

Discipline means setting clear boundaries for yourself and sticking to them. It means creating a routine or a plan of action, and committing to it, even when it's not easy or convenient. This might mean getting up early every morning to exercise or committing to a regular schedule of work, study or practice.

Commitment, on the other hand, means staying focused on your goals, even when there are distractions or obstacles in your way. It means making a promise to yourself to see things through, no matter what challenges you may encounter.

To cultivate these qualities within yourself, it's important to start small. Set small, achievable goals for yourself, and commit to them.

Once you've achieved these goals, set larger ones, and continue to push yourself outside of your comfort zone.

Never give up on your dreams. Remember that true personal excellence comes not from talent or intelligence, but from the willingness to work hard, to stay focused, and to stay committed to your vision. Always remember that you have the power within you to achieve greatness, if only you have the discipline and commitment to see things through.

Values and Principles

Few things are more important than our values and principles. These are the guiding lights that keep us on track, even in the face of adversity or temptation. For me, my values and principles were instilled in me from a young age, and they have been the cornerstone of my personal and professional life ever since. There are few things as powerful as having a clear sense of your values and principles and living your life in accordance with them. Values are the fundamental beliefs and attitudes that guide our behavior and decision-making. They are the things that we hold dear, and that give our lives purpose and meaning. Principles, on the other hand, are the rules and standards that we live by the code of conduct that governs our actions and interactions with others. In many ways your values and principles are entirely personal to you. They are shaped by your experiences, your beliefs, and your unique perspective on the world and that's why it's so important to take the time to identify your values and principles, and to live your life in accordance with them.

When you live your life in alignment with your values and principles, you will find that everything falls into place. You will have a clear sense of purpose and direction, and you will be able to make decisions with confidence and conviction. And even when faced with difficult choices or challenging situations, you will have a rock-solid foundation to fall back on. How can you identify your values and principles? Start by reflecting on what is most important to you. What are the things that you care deeply about, that give your life meaning and purpose? What are the principles that you hold dear, and that guide your interactions with others?

Once you've identified your values and principles, it's important to live your life in accordance with them. This means making conscious choices that reflect your values and holding yourself accountable for the principles that you've set for yourself. Values and principles are not set in stone. As you grow and evolve as a person, your values and principles may shift and change. The important thing is to always stay true to yourself, and to continue to live your life in alignment with your own personal code of conduct. I also want to emphasize that your values and principles should not just be theoretical concepts, but they should be reflected in your actions and behaviors. It's not enough to simply state that you believe in certain values or principles, you must demonstrate them through your actions. This is especially important in times of adversity or challenge. When things get tough, it's easy to abandon our values and principles in the pursuit of a quick fix or an easy way out. In fact, it is during these trying times that our values and principles are most important. They serve as a compass, guiding us towards the right course of action, even when the path is difficult or uncertain.

Courage, persistence, discipline, and commitment, which we have discussed before, all play a role in living a life in accordance with your values and principles. It takes courage to stand up for what you believe in, even when it's unpopular or difficult. It takes persistence to keep going, even when you encounter setbacks or obstacles. It takes discipline to stay true to your values and principles, even when you are tempted to compromise. It takes commitment to maintain your values and principles over the long haul, even in the face of adversity or temptation. Personal excellence is not just about achieving success, but about living a life of integrity and authenticity, in accordance with your own personal values and principles.

About the Author

Meet Noel Cox, a recognized expert in the aviation and aerospace industry with over 26 years of experience in airlines, airports, aviation consulting, and aircraft leasing. He is a published author of two books on mental transformation, "It's All in Your Mind" and "Being and Becoming the Art of Mental Transformation," recognized for their practical advice on developing the mindset and inner strength to succeed in both personal and professional life. As a pioneering wellbeing and lifestyle consultant for aviation and aerospace, Noel is dedicated to helping others reach their full potential. He has a proven track record of success in leadership, strategy, and innovation in many different commercial and operations areas. He coordinated the training of thousands of pilots at the biggest airline in Europe and is a sought-after aviation consultant with global clients. He also served for almost a decade in Latin America as Senior Commercial Relations Advisor to an airport authority senior management team in Central America. Noel's extensive career in the aviation industry began nearly three decades ago at the world's largest US airline where he also worked in various commercial and operational leadership roles for 14 years in their European Division. Before that, he worked in the United States with two other airlines in Massachusetts. With his vast aviation industry experience, expertise, and dedication to mental training and wellbeing, Noel is a sought-after consultant and a trusted guide to those seeking to achieve success in their personal and professional lives.

References

1. *Joan Cahill, Paul Cullen, Sohaib Anwer, Simon Wilson & Keith Gaynor (2021): Pilot Work Related Stress (WRS), Effects on Wellbeing and Mental Health, and Coping Methods, The International Journal of Aerospace Psychology, DOI: 10.1080/ 24721840.2020.1858714*
2. Ropp, T., Belt S., 2020 *Individual resilience as a competency for aviation professionals: A review of the literature.* 2020 ASEE Virtual Annual Conference
3. Bor, R., Eriksen, C., Oakes, M., & Scragg, P. (Eds). (2017). Pilot mental health screening and assessment. Ashgate Publications.
4. Sung, E., Chang , J., Lee S., Park, SH.(2019) The Moderating Effect of Cognitive Flexibility in the Relationship Between Work Stress and Psychological Symptoms in Korean Air Force Pilots. Military Psychology 31(4):1-7
5. Nicklas Dahlstrom & Staffan Nahlinder (2009) Mental Workload in Aircraft and Simulator During Basic Civil Aviation Training, The International Journal of Aviation Psychology, 19:4, 309-325, DOI: 10.1080/ 10508410903187547
6. Burke, C. S., Wilson, K. A., & Salas, E. (2003). Teamwork at 35,000 feet: Enhancing safety through team training. Human Factors and Aerospace Safety, 3(4), 287–312.
7. Herbert Benson, John F. Beary & Mark P. Carol (1974) The Relaxation Response, Psychiatry, 37:1, 37-46, DOI: 10.1080/ 00332747.1974.11023785
8. Santilhano, W., Bor, R., Hewitt M. 2019. The Role of Peer Support and Its Contribution as an Effective Response to Addressing the Emotional Well-Being of Pilots: A Qualitative Study of South African Stakeholders. Aviation Psychology

and Applied Human Factors 9(2):67-76 DOI:10.1027/2192-0923/a000163

9. Bauer, H., Herbig, B., 2019 Occupational Stress in Helicopter Emergency Service Pilots From 4 European Countries AirMed 38(2) DOI:10.1016/j.amj.2018.11.011
10. Venus, M., & grosse Holtforth, M. (2022). *Interactions of International Pilots' Stress, Fatigue, Symptoms of Depression, Anxiety, Common Mental Disorders and Wellbeing.* International Journal of Aviation, Aeronautics, and Aerospace, 9(1). DOI: https://doi.org/10.15394/ijaaa.2022.1667
11. Hiroki Murakami ,Takashi Nakao,Masahiro Matsunaga,Yukinori Kasuya,Jun Shinoda,Jitsuhiro Yamada,Hideki Ohira. 2012. *The Structure of Mindful Brain.* PLOS ONE. *https://doi.org/10.1371/journal.pone.0046377*
12. Cahill, J., Cullen, P. & Gaynor, K. The case for change: aviation worker wellbeing during the COVID 19 pandemic, and the need for an integrated health and safety culture. Cogn Tech Work 25, 75–117 (2023). https://doi.org/10.1007/s10111-022-00711-5
13. Katharine O Burleson 1, Gary E Schwartz. 2004. *Cardiac torsion and electromagnetic fields: the cardiac bioinformation hypothesis* DOI: 10.1016/j.mehy.2004.12.023

Tables

---

[1] Joan Cahill, Paul Cullen, Sohaib Anwer, Simon Wilson & Keith Gaynor (2021): Pilot Work Related Stress (WRS), Effects on Wellbeing and Mental Health, and Coping Methods, The International Journal of Aerospace Psychology, DOI:10.1080/24721840.2020.1858714

[2] Ropp, T., Belt S., 2020 Individual resilience as a competency for aviation professionals: A review of the literature. 2020 ASEE Virtual Annual Conference

[3] Bor, R., Eriksen, C., Oakes, M., & Scragg, P. (Eds). (2017). Pilot mental health screening and assessment. Ashgate Publications.

[4] Sung, E., Chang , J., Lee S., Park, SH.(2019) The Moderating Effect of Cognitive Flexibility in the Relationship Between Work Stress and Psychological Symptoms in Korean Air Force Pilots. Military Psychology 31(4):1-7

[5] Nicklas Dahlstrom & Staffan Nahlinder (2009) Mental Workload in Aircraft and Simulator During Basic Civil Aviation Training, The International Journal of Aviation Psychology, 19:4, 309-325, DOI: 10.1080/10508410903187547

[6] Burke, C. S., Wilson, K. A., & Salas, E. (2003). Teamwork at 35,000 feet: Enhancing safety through team training. Human Factors and Aerospace Safety, 3(4), 287–312.

[7] Herbert Benson, John F. Beary & Mark P. Carol (1974) The Relaxation Response, Psychiatry, 37:1, 37-46, DOI: 10.1080/00332747.1974.11023785

[8] Santilhano, W., Bor, R., Hewitt M. 2019. The Role of Peer Support and Its Contribution as an Effective Response to Addressing the Emotional Well-Being of Pilots: A Qualitative Study of South African Stakeholders. Aviation Psychology and Applied Human Factors 9(2):67-76 DOI:10.1027/2192-0923/a000163

[9] Venus, M., & grosse Holtforth, M. (2022). Interactions of International Pilots' Stress, Fatigue, Symptoms of Depression, Anxiety, Common Mental Disorders and Wellbeing. International Journal of Aviation, Aeronautics, and Aerospace, 9(1). DOI: https://doi.org/10.15394/ijaaa.2022.1667

[10] Hiroki Murakami ,Takashi Nakao,Masahiro Matsunaga,Yukinori Kasuya,Jun Shinoda,Jitsuhiro Yamada,Hideki Ohira. 2012. The Structure of Mindful Brain.

https://doi.org/10.1371/journal.pone.0046377

[11] Cahill, J., Cullen, P. & Gaynor, K. The case for change: aviation worker wellbeing during the COVID 19 pandemic, and the need for an integrated health and safety culture. Cogn Tech Work 25, 75–117 (2023). https://doi.org/10.1007/s10111-022-00711-5

[12] Katharine O Burleson 1, Gary E Schwartz. 2004. Cardiac torsion and electromagnetic fields: the cardiac bioinformation hypothesis DOI: 10.1016/j.mehy.2004.12.023

[13] Bauer, H., Herbig, B., 2019 Occupational Stress in Helicopter Emergency Service Pilots From 4 European Countries AirMed 38(2) DOI:10.1016/j.amj.2018.11.011

Don't miss out!

Visit the website below and you can sign up to receive emails whenever Noel Cox publishes a new book. There's no charge and no obligation.

https://books2read.com/r/B-A-WLKY-CBBJC

Printed in the USA
CPSIA information can be obtained
at www.ICGtesting.com
LVHW020900220324
775213LV00002B/244